NUDE WITH ATTITUDE
By Kay Hannam

NUDE WITH ATTITUDE

Published by Kaden Publishing
2704 State Highway 63
Wairau Valley RD1
Blenheim 7271, New Zealand
Tel: +64 3 5722681 ~ Email: info@naturist.co.nz
www.naturist.co.nz
First published in 2013
© Kay Hannam 2013
ISBN 978-0-473-23536-9

This book is copyright. Apart from any fair dealing for the purpose of private study, research, criticism or review, as permitted under the Copyright Act, no part of this publication may be reproduced, stored in a retrieval system, or transmitted in any form or by any means, electronic, mechanical, photo-copying, recording or otherwise, without prior permission of the publisher.

The moral rights of the author have been asserted.

Designed by Kay Hannam in conjunction with Blenheim Print.

Cover designed by Jarrid Bainbridge and Tom Bainbridge.

Cover photo by Scott Hammond and published with kind permission by Marlborough Express.

Printed and bound by Blenheim Print.

For Jackie

Nude with Attitude

Acknowledgements

Initially, a creative writing workshop in Timaru with Joan Rosier-Jones gave me the inspiration and confidence to begin writing, though the title had long been determined. It would be another ten years before I joined NZ Authors and availed myself of the amazing resources and services this organisation provides. Meeting the friendly members of the Top of the South Branch has been another bonus.

A Writers' Retreat led by Sally Astridge provided further inspiration and feedback, confirming I was on track and more importantly, my memoir was beginning to look and feel like a book. Dorothy Scott proof-read, edited and read the manuscript yet again with professional care and attention. Thank you, Dot, not only for your excellent advice and encouragement, but for your friendship and never ending cups of coffee. And in an endeavour to gain a 'family' perspective, I asked my niece, Mhairi Thompson, if she would critique it. Mhairi gladly accepted the challenge and read the draft manuscript during her holiday.

I am indebted to my friend Roger Fowler-Wright for the constant stream of information he gleefully and freely provides, although I know it is a distraction from his own busy life in London. I am extremely grateful for Roger's insightful and valuable inspiration.

NZNF Archivist and former National President, Les Olsen, was recently awarded Honorary Life Membership NZNF. I am honoured that Les agreed to write the foreword for my memoir.

My long association with both the New Zealand Naturist Federation and International Naturist Federation has provided me with many opportunities. I appreciate the support given by their executive and from members of the world wide naturist community. No memoir would be complete without photos and I wish to express my thanks to the individuals whose images feature in these pages.

I have dedicated this memoir to my beautiful daughter, Jackie, especially for her unconditional love, encouragement and understanding.

In addition to providing moral support; breakfast, lunch and dinner on many occasions; my loving partner, Brian Williams, deserves the biggest bouquet. Ever the problem solver, sometimes appreciated, sometimes not, Brian has continued to be my rock. None of this would have been possible without his dogged determination to provide the solutions and carry out the work required in order to fulfil the vision we share.

Contents

Foreword	11
Wear a Smile	13
The Bathing Suit	19
Trials and Tribulations	21
Skin is In	27
Moving On	33
Getting Involved	39
Hats are More Important than Pants	45
Blast from the Past	51
Promoting with Passion	57
Creating the Place to Be	61
From Casa Rosada to The White House	67
Scandinavian Adventure	71
That First Step	77
The Blue Dome of Freedom at Sweetwaters	83
Nude Zealand – Nationwide	87
The Beginning of an Endless Summer	91
A Taste of Europe	97
Sunhats and Shoes . . . Only	103
Alleys of Montemarte to Palais de Papes	109
Animals, Dead Ants and Dog-wallopers	115
Walk on The Wild Side	121
A Love Affair with Swiss Rail and Other Fast Trains	125

Dutch Treat	131
Four Workshops and a Wedding	135
Introducing Two Kiwis who can Fly	141
Mason Jars and the Devon Mafia	147
Croatia in the Buff	153
No Clothes Attached	157
World Naked Bike Ride	161
All Around the UK and More . . .	163
The Final Fling	169
The Bag Boy Goes to Europe	175
Spanish Hospitality	183
Life in the Valley	189
Up Tempo	191
Schnappshot of Hungary	193
Arrivals and Departures	199
Nude Nuptials	203
Nudie Foodies	207
Invitation to a Wedding – in France	211
Figure Studies	217
Naked Ambition	221
Life is Short – Play Naked	225
Festivals in France – Parks in Croatia	229
Nothing is Better	235

Nude with Attitude

And the weaver said, "Speak to us of Clothes."
And he answered:
Your clothes conceal much of your beauty, yet they hide not the unbeautiful.
And though you seek in garments the freedom of privacy you may find in them a harness and a chain.
Would that you could meet the sun and the wind with more of your skin and less of your raiment,
For the breath of life is in the sunlight and the hand of life is in the wind.
Some of you say, "It is the north wind who has woven the clothes to wear."
But shame was his loom, and the softening of the sinews was his thread.
And when his work was done he laughed in the forest.
Forget not that modesty is for a shield against the eye of the unclean.
And when the unclean shall be no more, what were modesty but a fetter and a fouling of the mind?
And forget not that the earth delights to feel your bare feet and the winds long to play with your hair.
Khalil Gibran - 'On Clothes' from 'The Prophet'

Nude with Attitude

Foreword

To review a book on one's lifestyle choice of nudity is somewhat daunting to the average person no doubt, but when someone's life experiences involve naturism over many years it is possible to reflect on their own life choices and find perspective in what they themselves have done.

In her book 'Nude with Attitude' Kay has outlined the many experiences she has enjoyed as a naturist, starting with her open attitude to nudity as a child, through the many life experiences and travel opportunities she has had as a lifelong devotee of the naturist experience.

Kay grew up in the South Island town of Timaru in a family of four siblings, three sisters and a brother and two portly parents, who had a very open attitude to nudity in the home. So much so that it was quite 'ho hum' to see her parents' nude frequently going about their daily ablutions.

Holidays in the countryside of South Canterbury provided further opportunities to be nude in the outdoors and frequently Kay would sneak out to go skinny dipping with friends when the occasion presented itself.

Her working life has given her frequent changes of job and broadened her outlook on life so much, so that her recent years have given her tremendous fulfilment in carrying on her naturist lifestyle, both on visits to European naturist destinations and in managing her nudist homestay initially in the McKenzie country and more recently in Marlborough with her partner Brian Williams.

She has been confident in engaging with the local community in accepting that nudity in the community is a worthy activity and recently won a business excellence award from the Marlborough Chamber of Commerce for her naturist park at *Wai-natur*.

Her forte is the promotion of naturism in New Zealand and her many appearances in the various news media have been helpful in generating interest throughout the country.

Nude with Attitude relates her nude adventures and is a proud testament to the lifestyle she and many others have chosen to live worldwide.

Les Olsen
Honorary Life Member NZNF

The Naturist – Kay Hannam. Reproduced from *With a Passion - The Extraordinary Passions of ordinary New Zealanders*. Photo by Stephen A'Court.

Wear a Smile

What's so special about taking your clothes off? My attitude is, if it's a nice day why put anything on except a hat and a pair of shoes where necessary. Wear a smile.

Most of us enjoy seeing young kids playing naked and free in the back yard with the neighbours, or at the beach. We've all got those baby photos in our albums to remind us of our own ecstatic squeals of delight as we, hesitant at first, lifted our little feet to avoid the cold and then dashed shamelessly into the shallows. It was a special feeling; one our parents wanted us to feel by not putting clothes on. I am continually reminded by proud parents and grandparents how their little ones love to be naked and hate clothing, yet they have no wish to experience this special feeling themselves.

It never occurred to me I might be considered as the one 'out of step' and have remained firm in my conviction pretty much all my life, that simply being nude is nothing to be ashamed of. As a family, getting dressed together in front of the fire after a bath or before school on a cold winter morning, was quite normal in our household; my mother calling to us on week days, 'for the last time, get out of bed and get dressed!' We would make a noisy bee-line for the lounge still warm in pyjamas, school clothes tucked under our arm before laying them on the hot grill of the oil-burner.

While others might recoil in shock/horror at the thought of one's super-sized father wandering down the hall from the bedroom to the bathroom wearing nothing but a singlet, my mother, also seriously on the tubby side, was pretty much the same. Neither bothered to cover up just because a door was open while getting dressed or undressed and I sensibly came to the conclusion that nudity was no big deal. There was no sense of false modesty, no sexual innuendo. Quite frankly I think my parents did me a big favour; never to feel ashamed of my body.

Even though I was the smallest and skinniest of our family (my father sometimes called me 'Bones'), my size and shape never bothered me. I was quite fit and healthy and have never suffered from any serious health issues.

Born 23 December 1946, in Timaru on the East coast of the South Island in New Zealand; my parents named me Kay Lucille Hannam. Why Lucille? The explanation was that Lucille was similar to our neighbour's name – Lucinda – 'anyway,' according to my father, 'it was better than being called Lucretia. She poisoned the Pope!'

In hospital during my pre-Christmas arrival, my mother would later reveal that one of the nurses had knitted and dressed me in a bright, multi-coloured, striped woollen jersey. It's no wonder clothes and I don't get along.

Born with what was termed a 'club foot', my mother underwent numerous operations on her leg until shortly after the age of 60, unable to eradicate acute Osteomyelitis, she had 'the damn thing off' and – with due predictability on her part – danced to *'Zorba the Greek'*, the following New Year's Eve.

Photographic records document the order of three sisters in quick succession following that of an older brother, each of us with three lettered names; Rex, Sue, Kay and Rae – which were never modified in any way – brought up in the same household together, completely different in personality and appearance; though my mother, who trained as a tailor in Christchurch and was a gifted dressmaker, endeavoured to dress us three girls as if we were triplets! As was the fashion back then.

Our family at Sue's 21st birthday party, Zingari Hall, Timaru. July 1966.

At the age of four, I became a pupil of the *Dorothy Thwaithes School of Dancing,* to learn ballet and tap-dancing. My mother's dressmaking skills were at their creative best during those ensuing six years, designing and sewing fluffy tutus and a seemingly never-ending variety of 'character' costumes, including a large number of *Coldstream Guards* costumes for the 52 members of the dancing school (all girls). Resplendent in smart black trousers seamed with satin stripe, bright red jacket, all the trimmings and topped with shiny black bearskins, in order of height (I was the second shortest); the entire contingent of the *Dorothy Thwaites School of Dancing* formed a guard of honour – at attention – either side of Stafford Street, during the 1954 visit to Timaru of Queen Elizabeth and the Duke of Edinburgh. Marjorie McKissock, on the opposite side, like me, was the second shortest and as we both stepped out for Marjorie to present Queen Elizabeth with flowers, I received a wink from the Duke!

The ballet dancer aged around 5

Born in another era, my mother would have been in her element competing in the World of WearableArt. She could always be relied on to come up with some dramatic fancy-dress outfit for me, whether it was held during the Caroline Bay Christmas Carnival or a local school fair. Even though I am comfortable about nudity, paradoxically, I still have a strong penchant for fancy-dress, with anything from a colourful harem costume to a witch's sombre flowing robes in my dress-up box.

Thanks to my mother's patient tuition, I also became adept at sewing and took great care about my appearance well into my adult life; paying special attention to the right look and colour – with varying shades of pink or red; burnt orange, lime green, though not necessarily what was in fashion at the time. One year I sported a pair of canary-yellow hot-pants with matching blouse trimmed with the same hot yellow!

Kay and Rex in fancy dress

In my younger childhood – during family outings at the weekend – I would frolic naked under the Skipton Bridge; and on Christmas holidays down south at a holiday bach in Karitane, near Dunedin, went skinny dipping with two young lads, Kerry and Richard, whose family home was next door.

Those early years were, in my view, the most memorable and happiest times of my childhood. Of course I was smitten with the younger boy, Richard, so it was an added attraction to play with 'the boys next door'.

As I understand it, my father had carried out some building alterations at the Excelsior Hotel in Timaru. The roomy bach was owned by the publican and we were lucky enough to spend two or three weeks there every summer until I was ten years old. A number of events happened that last year and I still have a very crooked arm to remind me.

We were all hoopin' and hollerin'; playing 'Cowboys & Indians' out in the neighbours' back yard. For whatever reason, Rex had tied a ladder onto a lawnmower which was lying hidden on the ground behind a large bush. Fearful of being 'scalped' by one of the marauding 'Indians', I (the 'squaw'), dived around the bush only to trip on this contraption and fall awkwardly on my elbow.

Naturally, I was cosseted and pampered, but it soon became obvious I had broken something. Next day we were all bundled into the car and were off over The Kilmog and Mt Cargill to Dunedin Hospital. Predictably, my younger sister threw up all over the pair of us, resulting in my admission wearing just a singlet and wrapped in an old grey woollen blanket. Afterwards, the rest of the family visited a department store to buy Rae a new dress. How unfair is that?

After an operation to remove the shattered radius head, my parents had to leave me to it and travelled back to Karitane with the rest of the family. A red-headed nurse came and told me off for crying. I was miserable.

Eventually, several days later, I was allowed to leave and the promise of a visit to the zoo lifted my spirits. How quickly that almost turned into another disaster, as the monkey I was so intent on giving my banana, decided my hair ribbon would look better on him. A sharp rap on the knuckles from my father's pipe soon changed his intentions.

Ballet lessons were now out of the question. Notwithstanding the fact that the term fees were now considered unaffordable; with my crooked arm I could no longer maintain a graceful en seconde.

My 'super-sized' father decided he had had enough of the building trade (well over 20 stone, he was too big anyway, and probably broke one ladder too many). Our lives changed when he bought a taxi. No more summer holidays in Karitane, no more skating trips to Lake Tekapo and calling in on the way home to visit Bram Lee at the Kimble Pub to enjoy raspberry drinks in the ladies lounge, no more weekend picnics to Skipton Bridge.

In spite of the early ballet lessons, I was considered the 'tomboy' in the family and fairly active. I tried hard at school, and was not really encouraged to participate in sport until, by my own volition, I joined the South End Swimming Club; rising during the early hours of most mornings for training before school. At best, I consider myself a bit of a plodder when it comes to swimming. Now, after all these years, I have my own pool and revel in the required number of lengths to complete my daily 'K' over the summer – naked of course!

Dad and 'Bluey' Coleman, both taxi owners, at a wedding in 1966

Caroline Bay was a favourite but fairly public haunt of mine. As a teenager, I would swim out to a raft anchored about 200 metres off shore; shed my bikini – securing it beneath the raft – while I swam in the deep safe waters, others completely oblivious to my nudity. Later I would lie naked, hiding in the dunes; the sun warming my body all over, blissfully and somewhat naively unaware of the meaning of the word sensuous, but in reality, discovering that feeling fairly early on in my life.

I just loved the water – still do, and for the most part conformed to society by wearing a bathing costume, particularly during my hours of training at the Century Pool. Although I was fairly competitive, those soggy togs never made me swim any faster!

Swimming is one of the many activities for which nudity is far more practical than clothing. Later, when I was in my early thirties, a group of us would regularly climb the fence of the old Century Pool in Craigie Avenue (before the roof went on) and experience the most delicious feeling –

skinny-dipping in the moonlight. The fact that this was deemed an illicit activity by some just added to the fun.

It always amuses me to witness others going through this inane towel dance in the pool changing rooms or at the beach. Much easier just to get your clothes off and be done with it. We were required to wear bathing costumes which had the effect of keeping us neither warm nor dry. It was all about modesty and what was socially acceptable, embedding the feeling of shame and poor body image as a result of these rigid rules.

The Bathing Suit

Only women and girls would really understand this. I would love to credit the author, but she chooses to remain unknown. She says,

'I have just been through the annual pilgrimage of torture and humiliation known as buying a bathing suit. When I was a child in the 1950's, the bathing suit for a woman with a mature figure was designed for a woman with a mature figure - boned, trussed and reinforced, not so much sewn as engineered. It was built to hold back and uplift and it did a good job.'

Today's stretch fabrics are designed for the prepubescent girl with a figure carved from a potato chip. The mature woman has a choice – she can either front up at the maternity department and try on a floral suit with a skirt, coming away looking like a hippopotamus who escaped from Disney's Fantasia – or she can wander around every run-of-the-mill department store trying to make a sensible choice from what amounts to a designer range of fluorescent rubber bands. What choice did I have?

I wandered around, made my sensible choice and entered the chamber of horrors known as the fitting room. The first thing I noticed was the extraordinary tensile strength of the stretch material. The Lycra used in bathing suits was developed, I believe, by NASA to launch small rockets from a slingshot, which gives the bonus that if you manage to actually lever yourself into one, you are protected from shark attacks. The reason for this is that any shark taking a swipe at your passing midriff would immediately suffer whiplash.

I fought my way into the bathing suit, but as I twanged the shoulder strap in place, I gasped in horror – my bosom had disappeared! Eventually, I found one bosom cowering under my left armpit. It took a while to find the other. At last I located it, flattened beside my seventh rib. The problem is that modern bathing suits have no bra cups. The 'mature woman' is meant to wear her bosom spread across her chest like a speed bump. I realigned my speed bump and lurched toward the mirror to take a full view assessment.

The bathing suit fitted all right, but unfortunately it only fitted those bits of me willing to stay inside it. The rest of me oozed out rebelliously from top, bottom, and sides. I looked like a lump of play dough wearing undersized cling wrap. As I tried to work out where all those extra bits had come from, the prepubescent sales girl popped her head through the curtains, 'Oh, there you are!' she said, admiring the bathing suit . . . I replied that I wasn't so sure and asked what else she had to show me.

I tried on a cream crinkled one that made me look like a lump of masking tape, and a floral two piece which gave the appearance of an oversized napkin in a serviette ring. I struggled into a pair of leopard skin bathers with a ragged frill and came out looking like Tarzan's Jane, pregnant with triplets and having a rough day. I tried on a black number with a midriff and looked like a jellyfish in mourning. I tried on a bright pink pair with such a high cut leg I thought I would have to wax my eyebrows to wear it.

Finally, I found a suit that fitted . . . a two piece affair with shorts-style bottom and a loose blouse-type top. It was cheap, comfortable, and bulge-friendly, so I bought it. My ridiculous search had a successful outcome! But, when I got home I found a label that said, 'Material will become transparent in water.' . . . !

Trials and Tribulations

As a youngster and well into my teens, I pushed the boundaries and, due to my parents' stern hand (at times fairly physical), it took me several years to recognise my own self esteem. I seemed to be constantly seeking approval because I was always being corrected.

Now I realise self worth is much more satisfying than someone else's validation.

Living in Victoria Street in the southern end of Timaru, meant we only had a short walk, and later a bike ride, to Main School, where all four of us completed our primary education. My father was pretty strict regarding whom I associated with. Even though we lived just a few blocks from the Catholic Basilica and school, back then 'doolies' were out! Association with ethnic alternatives were also discouraged.

Form 2, Timaru Main School. 1959. I am standing second from right in the third row from the front.

My education became an issue, and following a two year commercial course at Timaru Technical College, unable or unwilling to meet other's expectations, I dropped out of school and began employment in December 1962, as an office assistant at F. Lewis & Sons Ltd., Paint, Glass and Wallpaper Merchants. When I left 17 months later, I was informed I held the dubious distinction of having held the longest stay of an office junior.

For the next five years I worked in the office at Vibrapac, concrete block manufacturers situated at Washdyke on the outskirts of Timaru. Timaru Ready-mix Concrete was also produced there, and it was a good experience working in the building industry and, like many similar offices, I was the only female on the premises.

At my desk in the office at Vibrapac

Before long I had met Mr Right at a Caroline Bay Hall Dance, and on my 19th birthday became engaged to be married. All our spare time during the following year was spent building our home in Catherine Street, before marrying at Chalmers Church, in Timaru on 21st January 1967. My boss, Peter Mulholland, designed our home. Thanks to a generous staff discount and a day's work from my workmates, we made considerable savings on building costs.

I had made the commitment; later however, I determined something was not quite right with our relationship. After my children Moray and Jackie, were born, it was evident there were increasing irreconcilable differences. After seven frustrating years, I came to the conclusion that the Mr Right

Painting the roof of our new home in Catherine Street 1966

I married at twenty, was in fact Mr Wrong. The further frustration and stress of being a single parent of two very young children while working full time, seemed to wear at my very core. As a mother, I felt hopelessly inadequate and four years later, my children, in an endeavour to allow them greater opportunities, returned to live with their father, who by this time had remarried.

On reflection, 1978 was shaping up to be one of the best of my life. Two years earlier my children and I moved into our new home in Gleniti, on the corner of MacAulay Street and Springs Road and later Jackie began school. I applied for and accepted, the full-time position of receptionist at the Chateau Timaru, a licensed restaurant just a short distance from home, moonlighting as Maitre d' as and when required.

Our treasure, a 70 year old grandmother, would arrive at 3pm to meet my children at home from school, play with them, bring in the washing, do the ironing, and cook dinner. By the time I arrived home, shortly after 6pm, my children were fed and bathed, ready for bed. My own dinner would be in the oven. Wow! What a treasure!

Life was on track until later that year. One by one I said goodbye to each of the employees; chefs, kitchen hands, waitresses, cleaners, gardener, even the manager, until finally it was my turn, following a mortgagee sale. The business, through no fault of my own I might add, went bankrupt. Those of you who have lived in Timaru may know of the financial history of The Chateau, but it was quite unfortunate the new owner was unable to keep the business financially viable. Not only did I feel guilt-ridden by my children's absence, I was feeling even more inadequate than before.

In an endeavour to meet the running costs of my home and now maintenance payments, I advertised for a boarder to supplement my part-time employment. It was a bit of trial and error, with the first occupant running up some horrendous telephone bills. A second advertisement brought a knock on the door from a rather handsome man with greying hair.

My first impression of John Clayton, apart from his twinkling blue eyes, was his nonchalant stance on the bottom step of the back door. Well in excess of six foot, John confided to me later that it was a salesman's ploy, to appear less-threatening to the house-holder. To say I didn't feel threatened would be straying from the truth somewhat. At the risk of turning this chapter into Mills & Boon genre, my knees turned to blancmange and with palpitating heart, I invited him in for a chat. The chemistry between us was electric and it became evident I should continue to look for a paying boarder. I wanted, he wanted, much more. This man was definitely not boarder material!

A nurse by the name of Chris, eventually bagged the boarder's bedroom. We called him Kristoff, and he was such a lot of fun – gay being the operative word. John, now my significant other, would travel down from Christchurch where he was living and working at the time, and the three of us would often go out pubbing together.

However the drama of Kristoff's relationships got completely out of hand in the early hours of one morning when his male lover tried to axe my back door open. Kristoff had to go!

Friends Denise and Len Te Koeti and their family lived in the house next door, in Springs Road. It was Denise, at the time working in the display advertising department (known as the A-Team), of *The Timaru Herald*, who put in a good word for me, suggesting I apply for a vacancy in the classified section of the newspaper.

During the next five years I worked alongside my new friends and workmates, Ann Marshall and Liz Crawford, accepting classified advertisements over the telephone and typing them up on forms. It was 1980 and the convoluted process of producing a newspaper was undergoing radical change. Within the first twelve months, we three clerical workers were transferred from our cupboard in the old Herald building in Sophia Street, into a spacious, re-furbished two storied building in Bank Street nicknamed Fawlty Towers. Our iconic Imperial 66's were replaced with computers, and negotiations succeeded in our acceptance by the printers union.

I was in my element! It was hectic and extremely stressful adapting to the new technology, while at the same time, frantically typing up advertising content toward deadlines on Thursdays and Fridays. On these days our classified crew was increased by another two telephonists. Not only did we have a stack of hard copy from customers coming in off the street to the office downstairs, but the telephones were constantly ringing, with anything from the sale of lounge suites to funeral notices. All required a calm voice responding to their needs and attention to detail.

There was a down time, during which I composed poems about other staff members in the advertising and paste-up sections. I was a great fan of Pam Ayers, and was given the pen name Kaos, Hon Member for putting on Ayers. Nobody was safe from my cryptic quips as my two cohorts and many others on the top floor, gave plenty of encouragement and ideas to send up somebody for just having a birthday, expecting a child, or worse – leaving us all!

Trials and Tribulations

Part-time Grind

Oh Betty, What is it we have done to make you want to go?
I've tried to guess just what it is, I hope it's not B.O.

Perhaps it is the massive task of moving over there,
or is it 'cause you once reclined in the fated Preggy Chair?

Now Betty here, she's been around the 'Hallowed Herald Halls'
Eight years or more she's found a niche within those wondrous walls.

This lass has had a part-time job beyond your wildest dreams,
she's made herself available all o'er the place it seems

From office desk and telephone, she made her merry way,
to become a star and good friend too of the team that starts with A.

A Jack of all trades, master of none, oh that's not really fair,
she's very good at laying out and her typing is pretty fair.

The C-team, that's us Classified, oh yes, we've had her too,
but when we switched to VDT's, the Union said to shoo!

Up she popped again, is there no holding this girl down?
Another desk, another job, she hasn't even left town.

I'm sure if Ray B said to her, 'I have to go away,
my office will be empty, would you like to come and play?'

For some months now she's found the time to mark the Saturday rag,
scribbling all over with coloured pens, she's really quite a dag.

'Now where's this ad, why is it not in?' she marches in the door.
'Don't worry Betty; it wouldn't fit, so they dropped it on the floor'.

'Oh, will we credit or compensate, will we just wait and see?
He may not notice it's not there – let's have a cup of tea'.

You'll note there have always been one or two spare chairs,
the sudden truth that now there's none, has brought her close to tears.

For on the move to 'Fawlty Towers', our Betty had a fit,
'I've looked around and I cannot find, a place for me to sit!'

'No 'Fawlty Towers' for me', she says, 'I'll not sit around and moan.'
So off she goes to buy herself a building of her own.

A month to find the where-with-all and now it seems she's set
to move in, husband, boys and all, there's hope for Betty yet.

No more for her the part-time grind above and below the stairs,
nor will she have the time to sit, upon our bloody chairs.

The time has come to wish her luck as she goes out the door,
You'll find her somewhat permanent at Motel Ambassador.

Foreman Gary Kitto, also president of the staff social club, may have had some insight into my business acumen as I was given the task of buying and selling veggies from the local auctioneer. We didn't have Excel spreadsheets in those days. Nonetheless, armed with a large piece of cardboard headed up *Kaos Co-op* and a variety of fruit and vegetables to choose from, written in orderly fashion across the top, I set about encouraging other staff members to support our social club initiative. In those days more than 300 staff worked for the Herald, so it was a pretty select group who received the goods and a wonderful opportunity for me to meet and get to know other people, including Managing Director, Ray Bennett, who, at that time, was Mayor of Timaru and a regular customer.

Answering the telephone with a smile for *The Timaru Herald*, Photo *The Timaru Herald*.

Bagging the increasing amount of produce each Thursday morning meant arriving at work an hour earlier and, even though I usually had plenty of help from my co-workers, it was a mad scurry in the locker room to get the job done before the phones started ringing.

Routinely, every second weekend, Moray and Jackie would come to stay in our home at Gleniti, ensuring family and neighbourhood relationships were maintained.

My mother was an absolute rock during this time and often acted as intermediary to solve recurring problems. Life wasn't exactly in the fast lane, but it was as balanced as it could be under the circumstances.

A sixty-a-day cigarette addiction had finally got the better of my father and, after a couple of heart attacks no doubt brought about by his lungs collapsing, a severe stroke left him paralysed down his right side. The taxi he was driving was a complete write-off, but his weight saved him. My mother, with her own health problems, had her leg amputated the following year and was to endure the next seven years looking after Dad without home help, before he died in hospital. Sadly, Mum died at the age of 72 after a long battle with leukaemia.

Honesty, kindness and strength came easily to my mother.

Skin is In

Surprisingly, one of my long term interests from the age of fourteen involved pipe bands. I had never expressed interest in playing a musical instrument, but it was apparent I had good rhythm. A number of neighbourhood friends at the time played the bagpipes and encouraged me to join the *Timaru Ladies' Pipe Band* as a side drummer.

Mum and Dad were especially supportive (I guess they knew the discipline would keep me out of trouble). Before long Mum was on the Committee, enjoying as many long lasting friendships as I did. It was a busy time in my life, trying to fit in girl guides, roller skating and swimming. Once a week we met for drumming practice in the old Toc H rooms in Sophia Street. Saturday mornings, particularly nearing contest time, would be spent doing drill practice at one of several parks around the city, learning the quickstep. Initially just learning to march and play at the same time was quite a feat.

Often, particularly in the summer, the band would parade at various community events; the most significant being when the Queen Mother visited Timaru and the ladies band marched down Stafford Street and stood to attention outside the Theatre Royal, as her majesty arrived for a civic function.

For the next couple of decades or more, I became adept at flams, drags and paradiddles. After a few years I progressed to the rank of Drum Major,

Above: Drum-Major leading the Timaru Ladies Pipe Band; Below: City of Timaru Highland Pipe Band.

proudly leading the band on parade. Each year Provincial contests were held and occasionally we competed in national contests at Grade 4 level. I was later invited to join *The City of Timaru Highland Pipe Band* (the men's band). This was a Grade 2 band which meant I had to step up a few notches. It was certainly challenging.

I loved the camaraderie of pipe bands, and attending several national and provincial band contests, were certainly highlights on the band calendar. My girlfriend, Heather King and I, had some great social times together at these events, even when we were not competing. And, as I am wont to do, some of those memorable and humorous events were recorded in history.

The Band from Manawatu

It were a March Friday that we set off
Dunedin here we come.
The Pipe Band Champs was our foremost aim
and of course a bit of fun
The skirl of pipes and the beating of drums
set our adrenalin flowin',
With medleys, street march, quicksteps and all,
these made our faces a glowin'
Oh how we all cheered that day in the stands
Invercargill were No. 1
And the Caley Ladies were jumpin' and shoutin'
'Look out men, here we come!'
The City Hotel was the venue for lunch
A beer to wash it down
Old friends we met, some new ones too.
By bus we left the town.
T'was quite a repertoire they had
Songs, sung proper too
We thanked them all, thought what a great crew
The band from Manawatu.
Two days were past and all was well,
Then down to the old Town Hall
There we all were boozin' and dancin'
and having a helluva ball.
With the clock at one we then departed
Bound for the City Hotel
There to continue our boozin' and singin'
The night was a pup – what the hell!

Young Squinty recited a poem or two
And kept us all in fits
They carried on singing and most of the songs
Were naughty in little bits

'We've had a great time,' said the fella beside me
'I'd like to go – wouldn't you?'
By the arm I was led, away to his bed
To do whatever you do

It were all about over and we were in clover
When hark! A knock at the door!
We tried to ignore it but hadn't a chance
For they were a-knockin' some more

A balding pervert let them in
Him, with the master key
Through the door, the windows too
They all came in to see

They turned on the light and burst into song
I thought, it's bloody well true
They've got no Fallorum and bugger all dicdorum
the Band from Manawatu

Now we have two years to plan our revenge
It won't be just apple-pied beds
Oh sorry they'll be when they leave Timaru
With their tails between their legs

We'll get that band of minstrels
And on our own patch too
We'll get them all, the ones they call
The band from Manawatu

Pipe bands continued to retain my interest for twenty-five years and so decision time, endowed in woollen kilt and feather bonnet, plus all the trimmings, meant I went from being heavily into clothes into being heavily out of them. Skin was in!

Being aware of that special feeling of freedom, the caress of water and kiss of sun and air all over my body, stayed with me into adulthood. I was not one to go through a stage, so it was not surprising that as a young mother I determined that it was perfectly natural for my own children to swim and play naked.

Our weekend jaunts, sometimes with John along as well, would often find us skinny-dipping after our picnic lunch at Stratheona River, near Pleasant Point. The pleasure of bouncing down the Otira River in a tyre tube, the kids screaming their heads off with excitement (or was it fear), was anticipated long before we headed up the Point Road.

Before long we found the local sun club with its rustic grounds, just over the stop bank, which naturally whetted our curiosity to find out more.

More came in the form of *Pineglades*, established as the *Canterbury Sun & Health Club* at Rolleston, in the early fifties. To say that I took to it like a duck takes to water would be an understatement.

After jumping the locked gate, and confidently fronting up to the sea of brown bodies, John and I were invited by the friendly membership secretary to 'pull up a bit of grass and enjoy the sunshine'. That was okay for a while, but I was keen to locate the swimming pool. Once found, it took me all of six seconds to get my clothes off and into the water.

Needless to say we became members and returned to *Pineglades* on a regular basis. Within a few weeks we found an old banger (a large Retro caravan) to renovate. Arrangements were underway to spend our annual summer holidays at *Pineglades*.

But first to convince the children!

'Remember when we found the place with all the trees just over the stop bank at Pleasant Point, and we had a picnic with all the other families?' I soothed. 'Well, we have found something even better, near Christchurch and we would like you to join us in the caravan there, for a couple of weeks during the school holidays. There's a large swimming pool, children's play area and a forest where you can build huts. Of course there will be loads of families there with young children. The best thing is, you won't have to wear clothes'

'I think we had better discuss this,' asserted Moray to his young sister. So off they went to his bedroom, closing the door, cackling and giggling. Before long they were back. Moray resolutely informing me, 'Well, we would like to go, but we're not going to tell Dad!'

'I don't think that's a very good idea' was my immediate response, 'I think you should tell him'.

'Nope,' said Moray, 'he wouldn't understand.' He was correct of course, his father never did get a handle on nudity, his own or anyone else's for that matter.

Of course, our holiday and subsequent visits with the children to *Pineglades* were a great success. *Pineglades* had everything, and still does. Sports courts, large club lounge and bar, ablution blocks, children's play area, swimming pool, spa & sauna, numerous baches (or cabins), and camping areas. Covering 18 acres, the grounds are beautifully landscaped, with plenty of shelter, quite private and secure.

If I didn't know about nudism or naturism then, it didn't take me long to catch on and realise just how something so simple could be so good for my own health and wellbeing. There was this incredible liberation. A feeling of I'm OK and you're OK. Many, women in particular, would call it a feeling of empowerment.

Sure, I felt a moment of trepidation taking that first step into the swimming pool. But it was just a moment. Walking naked across the grounds bereft of sarong was an even bigger moment, but not insurmountable. After all, everyone else was doing the same and nobody was taking any notice. They may have taken more notice if I had been fully clothed.

Tony Nee was one of those people that went out of his way to make us all feel welcome, and has remained a good friend over the years. Like many other members of the club, Tony and his family lived in Christchurch, arriving Friday nights after work to stay in their caravans at *Pineglades* almost every weekend during the summer. We all enjoyed a wonderful camaraderie as we very quickly made new friends, with plenty of sport and social activities to suit all ages and interests.

In the same manner as I enjoyed an easy familiarity with my parents, my children and their new friends were not curious about other peoples' bodies. Given the opportunity to grow up in a non-threatening naturist environment such as *Pineglades*, the children had a better understanding and acceptance of other body shapes and sizes and how they develop. When children play happily together naked and are familiar with people of all ages, they are free from that silliness around older people and have a healthy attitude to those of the opposite sex.

The whole thing becomes natural for them – as they are too busy having a good time and being children. We can be assured they are safe, in fact children are far safer in a naturist environment than many children walking to school. Because everyone is looking out for one another, like a big family, everyone can get on with the business of relaxation, a world away from the stresses of everyday life.

By relaxation, I don't mean just lying around taking in the sun all day. An appointed sports convenor would draw up a comprehensive calendar of sporting and social activities for us to participate in over the summer. We were never bored. Even a cup of afternoon tea became a social occasion and before long we knew just about everyone in the club by name.

One of the funniest 'moments' came a few months later during a *Top Town* type competition, run much in the same manner as *It's a Knockout*. Only this was a knockout with a difference!

Players hoisted another, lighter player onto their shoulders, to attack the opposite team with rolled up wet newspapers. I found myself hoisted aloft Tony's broad shoulders. He probably never gave it a thought, but to me, the newbie, sitting naked astride his neck, hanging on for dear life, warding off the opposing team with a limp wet newspaper was an experience I will never forget. I nearly fell off laughing.

Moving On

In 1986, after having lived all my life in Timaru, it was time to consider my future direction. Due to John's influence and the acceptance I had gained as a person at *Pineglades*, I now enjoyed the confidence to make some significant changes to my lifestyle, which, let's face it, needed another rev.

Door to door selling might not be everyone's cup of tea and is not something I would eagerly contemplate nowadays. I learnt the system very quickly, having dabbled in selling life insurance previously. In fact the first house I checked out in need of the wonder covering *Super Shield*, a two pot epoxy mix suitable for concrete floors and steps, resulted in a sale and my first commission!

Eventually, though somewhat reluctantly, I relinquished my full-time position at *The Timaru Herald* and was given a resounding Scottish send-off by staff members, several penning their own rhymes in retaliation for the previous five years of Kaos.

Ode to Kaos

It may be said in any state
Your skill with words is simply great
But only time will tell the tale
When lost for lines or rhymes that fail
You finally need a helping hand
And who better than the whole Pipe Band.
For wit galore and stories rummy
These haggis munchers are quite funny
And though the need for censorship remains
And comments unkind should be restrained
You'll still come through with a laugh or two
Without resort to anything blue.
So now you've changed your job it seems
From what was once a land of dreams
To coatings for this and coatings for that
And all sorts of products, we know not what
So here's to you for ever more
Your future undoubtedly, is on the floor.

I then relocated north to live and work in Christchurch, having first rented out our home in Gleniti. One of the baches at Pineglades had come up for sale, and was to become my home away from home off and on for several years.

This photo was taken while celebrating Heather's birthday in Christchurch 1995.

Heather and I had earlier made a pact that we would attend the Edinburgh Military Tattoo before we were forty. Time was up and plans were underway. As it turned out, Heather was unable to travel due to family commitments and it was with some trepidation I decided to go alone, having been encouraged by a local travel agent friend to, 'explore Europe with a Trafalgar coach tour and visit twenty-two cities in twenty-eight days, followed by a two week round trip of the UK, taking in the Edinburgh festival and other special highlights'.

I would have been quite happy to fly directly to Edinburgh and return home following the festival. Looking back of course, there were some lasting and memorable moments in Europe: Climbing the Eiffel Tower and, somewhat less confidently, the Leaning Tower of Pisa. Witnessing sombre Yugoslavia; revelling in music and dancing in Athens and remembering with poignant significance, my mother's love for Greek culture; colourful impressions of the Netherlands, Belgium, France, Germany and Switzerland; floating in the Bari Sea. Italy held me in its spell, in awe of the Coliseum and titillated by erotic Pompei, with an unforgettable experience of buying a stunning hot pink dress in Sorrento, which I refuse to dispose of after all these years, having being fitted by two delightful assistants at 10:30pm in the evening!

I was the only Kiwi on the tour and shared a room with Marilyn, an older American woman. Like myself, Marilyn had never travelled to Europe and we enjoyed some good experiences together. It also meant there was someone to take the obligatory photo. The trip was not without incident, with an Italian woman on the tour screaming blue murder at the tour director and coach driver, in fact anyone she took a dislike to. It was pretty alarming at times, but they seemed to be unable or unwilling to do anything about her.

Security was always an issue and we were warned to take extra special care in known trouble spots, particularly in and around Rome. This advice was ignored completely by a couple of Australian girls, who consequently had their bags virtually knifed off their shoulders by speeding motorcyclists.

I recalled the chagrin and disbelief expressed by the girls a number of years later, when my laptop was snatched as some of London's low-life hassled me on the underground, the strapping holding my luggage together, smartly separated by their accomplices with a sharp knife.

Marilyn and I watched out for one another and returned to London with our luggage intact.

Imagine my disbelief when checking in at the London office four days later for the next coach tour, to learn that my travel agent had not reserved a ticket to the tattoo! Good grief! This was the whole point of going in the first place! Undaunted, I contacted the Tattoo ticket office myself. Luckily it was possible to purchase a ticket for one of the two nights we were due to stay in Edinburgh.

By the time the coach tour arrived in the north of Scotland, more than half the tour group had expressed a wish to attend the tattoo also. I managed to purchase tickets for them all on my Visa and charged each a percentage, then had a stand-up fight in the elevator with the tour director who demanded a commission! Needless to say, I told her where to get off.

Firmly etched in my memory would be sitting atop the Scottish capital's ancient castle in the pouring rain, totally enthralled by the *Massed Pipes and Drums of the Scottish Regiment* marching across the drawbridge. The line-up for the spectacular event also included the first military band from Germany to perform in the tattoo, the *Boys Brigade*, with an entertaining display of broom drill, *Pipes and Drums of the Argyll* and *Sutherland Highlanders of Canada*, and *King Edward VII's Own Gurkha Rifles*. The finale of *The Black Bear*, my favourite Scottish tune, brought me to tears. It was worth all that money to witness this world famous spectacle.

Travelling overseas was a real eye-opener and created a greater awareness for me regarding other countries and cultures. But I loved New Zealand and had no wish to travel again, particularly after arriving home in September and driving through Hagley Park, ablaze with daffodils, the glistening Southern Alps only a few hours away. New Zealand has such spectacular and unique scenery and I am very fortunate to have visited and lived in some of the best, though there is still a great deal on my bucket list yet to see. Little was I to know I would eventually return to many of these wonderful countries on several occasions, in years to come.

Back home to *Pineglades* and reality set in with a thump: a very large credit card bill to address, a pressing requirement to buy a decent car, plus an extra mortgage to fund the bach. Mindful of the recent death of my sixty-a-day father, the cigarettes had to go. 31st October 1986 was the date set in my diary to allow time to try hypnotherapy, acupuncture and other deterrents, none of which worked. In the end attitude won and it was 'cold turkey'.

Selling *Super Shield* on behalf of franchisees was going reasonably well, but was fraught with problems beyond our control, so we turned to aluminium joinery, selling on behalf of a newly formed company, *Regency Aluminium*. It was then I bought my very first computer, an Amstrad, and taught myself how to use it. I was training my own sales team by this time, having formed a company named *Kayl Marketing*. One of my friends at *Pineglades* introduced me to SWAP (Salesman With A Purpose), and I soon found myself getting up at the crack of dawn every Tuesday morning for their breakfast meeting, joining the early morning chorus, 'I'm alive, I'm well, and I feel great!'

My relationship with John ended. I was devastated.
  The impulse to burst into tears would hit me sporadically throughout the day, every day. Soon afterwards my sales team departed, enticed by the competition with the lure of fringe benefits that never actually eventuated. It was a cut-throat world, but my attitude was that life is as good as what you put into it and I soon joined another well established aluminium joinery company. Following the system, doing the numbers, but without the risk and without any personal involvement ensured that I remained focused on the job in hand.
  Even though I was working hard and achieving good sales, I was still on an emotional roller-coaster. On the surface I appeared confident and in control and although content to live alone, I lacked motivation to grow and become a better person. In order to move on completely, I needed to get rid of the demons of relationships past.

Jackie continued to enjoy long term friendships with several other nudie kids into her teenage years, taking the bus after school from Timaru to Rolleston every second Friday and returning Sunday evening, *Pineglades* being a little over a kilometre from the bus stop. On several occasions during the summer, we would visit other clubs around the country together. We both made some great friends and enjoyed a unique social atmosphere not found elsewhere.

More importantly, it was somewhere safe and secure for Jackie and me to benefit from a feeling of wellbeing many others spend hundreds of dollars trying to emulate. There's a lot of truth in the expression, 'you shed your stress when you shed your clothes'.

Our new friends John and Jane Meredith and their three young boys, the eldest Jackie's age, lived within walking distance of *Pineglades* and had visited the grounds a number of years earlier during a Club open day. The Merediths determined the lifestyle was a good fit for them and eventually built a large bach at *Pineglades* in order to live there.

Although not living on the grounds, a couple from Hornby with three young girls, again much the same age as Jackie, visited *Pineglades* most weekends. Together with Tony's family, we adults and children alike, formed a strong bond and there were often tears all round when each of the children went their separate ways, following the Sunday night barbecue.

My bach at *Pineglades* provided a wonderful retreat and I enjoyed the company of many friends. I missed my children terribly when they were with their father, particularly Jackie, but knew that to dwell on something I could do nothing about was not going to help.

I read innumerable books on the subject of personal motivation and to find out what inspires people to change their work/life patterns. It was inevitable that I found myself thinking about the meaning of Inspiration and Motivation and learnt if inspiration is about feeling, then motivation is about being moved to action. The two terms are often used together and sometimes interchangeably, and no wonder! In order to motivate someone, you have got to first make them feel an emotion and the emotion they feel can be so strong it encourages them to take action.

It was through my contacts at SWAP I learned about *Dale Carnegie Training*, which would, if I applied myself correctly, produce a behavioural change. The course which spanned several weeks, covered aspects on becoming a more effective communicator and developing human relationship skills, both essential tools which would become useful in both my professional and personal life.

Nude with Attitude

Getting Involved

Inevitably I became immersed in committee affairs at *Pineglades*, my nomination for social convenor somehow getting confused with that of secretary. Unlike my mother, I had not had much experience of committee work, but being a trained office administrator did have its advantages. A few jaunts around the country attending annual national rallies, and before long, I found myself co-opted onto the organising committee for the following, and subsequent, national rallies, hosted by *Pineglades*.

These annual rallies or naturist festivals were, and still are, held after Christmas, for a period of six or seven days. Following the *New Zealand Nudist Federation*, now known as the *New Zealand Naturist Federation* (NZNF) Annual General Meeting and a Grand Opening Ceremony, several sports tournaments which are hotly contested, get underway. Ankle-biters are not forgotten, with their own special activities created by a group of dedicated parents, to keep them occupied for hours at a time.

A large marquee is usually hired for indoor sports such as table tennis and darts and for entertainment provided in the evenings. This can be anything from a theatre restaurant, to jazz concerts or hypnotist shows, and a special themed New Year's Eve party with live band – the highlight of the week. Club members who take on the task of organising these annual events, do so voluntarily and are a great way of bringing club members and other visitors from around New Zealand and overseas together.

I very nearly didn't take part in my first ever Annual Rally, as the general discussion that took place when I was in Nelson at the time, prior to the forthcoming event, was quite negative. This, as I was to learn later, was nothing but 'club politics'.

We all had a blast, including Jackie! The *O.K. Rally*, with a cowboy theme, drew several hundred club members and visitors from all over New Zealand to *Pineglades*. Of course I was roped in to take part in the club's concert item, dressed as a saucy saloon girl, complete with red & black bustier, suspender belt with black stockings, and not much else. I'll never forget hearing my daughter's voice emanating from the group of youngsters sitting in front of the stage, with the lines of a well known television commercial, 'Oh look! That's my mother, the one with the wrinkly panty-hose.'

Sloppy, slippery, outrageous top team games during the lunch hour, were a great way of getting everyone involved with anything from apple bobbing, the slippery slide, and raft races. Yes, build your own team raft and manoeuvre it around the grounds before launching in the swimming pool. Points were accrued and totalled at the end of the rally, with the winning team being presented with the grand trophy. Even though they were supposed to be a fun event, to give us non-sporty types and youngsters the opportunity to participate, we nevertheless put everything into winning for our club.

New Year's Day and the annual swimming regatta was on the programme, with best swimming style, underwater races, age competitions and team relays encouraged by vocal supporters around the perimeter of the pool. Adults and children alike had a tremendous time and before the week long festivities were concluded, plans were being made to get together the following year.

Wellington was to be the venue for the next rally with a nautical theme planned. Jane and I had plenty of time to get ourselves and others enthused and twelve months later, forty-two red & black clad, one-eyed Cantabrians, aged from two to sixty two, shouldering stuffed parrots and brandishing cardboard cutlasses, stormed down the hill at Te Marua and ambushed the meticulously catered breakfast prepared by the catering crew.

King Neptune made a lunchtime appearance the next day and during the inevitable 'crossing the line ceremony', one of our inveterate pirates was trussed and consigned to the 'sea'.

In contrast, the afternoon's Jazz concert provided by the *Valley Stompers* was a hilarious experience, as we mingled on the lawn, dancing naked with gay abandon, to talented musicians playing many of our favourite dance tunes.

New Year's Eve celebrations were themed on a Hawaiian Luau, which made dressing up for the evening colourful, and relatively easy, after all some of us simply wore a sarong and a floral lei with many discarding the sarong for just the lei as the evening warmed up! The food was sumptuous to say the least, with the Wellington catering crew pulling out all stops to feed the hundreds of visitors.

With the usual depth of talent present, the concert was held with a choice variety of items.

Bevan Tong - an accomplished cornet player – and I performed our own haunting rendition of *Lili Marlene*

> *Underneath the yard-arm by the galley door*
> *Darling I remember the way you begged for more*
> *'Twas there 'neath the mainsail we did sweat*
> *You said I'll bet we'll get there yet*
> *My sailor from the Mainland, my Mainland sailor boy*
> *Time would come for roll call time for us to part*
> *You would swing your anchor I'd try not to laugh*
> *I saw your blue peter hanging there*
> *And you so bare a view so rare*
> *My sailor from the Mainland, my Mainland sailor boy*

When we weren't being entertained, or entertaining others, we were vocally supporting competitors on the sports courts, chiefly volleyball, tennikoits or miniten, a game similar to tennis, played on a smaller court, all of which were fiercely contested.

This week long rally gave me more insight into the depth of talent naturist clubs have, and *Wellington Naturist Club*, as it is now known, is no exception. Their organising committee had even built a boat to house the bar! Of course the captain was made to walk the plank, prodded by one of our parochial pirate gang. The event would forever go down in naturist history as the *Pirates Rally*.

I had previously shied away from competitive activities. I just didn't know how to play, and, being over forty, didn't feel confident about beginning. All that changed when I was introduced to miniten, and once I got a grip on using the wooden bat or thug, as it was called, Jane and I would lark around on the No. 2 court away from the critical eyes of the miniten guns.

Serving on the miniten court.

The following Christmas, Jackie and I flew to Auckland, the City of Sails. I shared a caravan with Norm and Beryl Wilkinson for the duration of the rally while the youngsters pitched tents. The Wilkinson family were quite sporty, as were several other Cantabrians, who made the journey especially to take part in as many sports competitions as time would allow.

We were all there to have some fun and it was Norm who came up with the idea to highjack the official Opening Ceremony with the sacrificial Canterbury lamb, in this case Hugh McCaw, wrapped in sheepskin and hog-tied to a pole, ceremoniously brought to the slaughter by two handsome nude Greek athletes (Norm's sons). I don't remember the lines, but do recall being one of the vestal virgins who cast the lamb's entrails into the bloodthirsty crowd.

Some weeks earlier, our committee had appointed me as their delegate for the NZNF AGM. The person originally given the task had decided not to attend. I was confused with her, as she and I shared the same first name and she, unbeknown to me, was apparently quite unpopular. First I had to convince others I was me and not she, but worse, I was to lobby other delegates to support the Canterbury Sun Club's decision not to host the rally the following year. I didn't agree with their stance at all, but as their delegate, I was compelled to support it. As it turned out, the following rally was held at the *Manawatu Outdoor Leisure Club*, now known as the *Manawatu Naturist Club*, and was a credit to their organising team. Practically the whole tribe of Indians, aka club members, were involved in the running of the rally.

By this time I had the miniten disease, and started playing in competitions for the very first time, having spent every prior spare moment on the court sharpening up my game.

Pineglades 1991 and I had the job of Rally Secretary. Norm, as Dr Who'N coerced all and sundry to get involved, including the local Dialek, who, thanks to remote control, totally mystified the ankle-biters and several adults among us. When we weren't playing miniten, ten of us had been rehearsing our specially choreographed dance routine and planning our costumes. No wrinkly pantyhose on this occasion!

Resplendent with luminous shocking pink or lime green lightning bolts painted on our bodies, with white boots and amulets, long varnished talons and sparkling OTT headgear, our entrance, preceded by dry ice steaming from the red telephone box, brought screams from the audience. Even more screams as we went through our opening routine to the famous Rocky Horror legend, *The Time Warp*.

Getting Involved

Again and again, the tune would be broadcast over the sound system during the next few days, and of course we would all stop what we were doing, adults and children alike, and do *The Time Warp*. Of course doing it in the nude just added to the fun.

But the serious fun was to be found on the miniten courts. I found myself through the early rounds of the Ladies Doubles, aided in no small measure by my partner Beryl. A similar scenario eventuated with the mixed doubles. Stanton Burrows was a long time member of the club and a damn good miniten player for his age. With these two on my end of the court when it mattered, I was gaining confidence and court craft, plus a unique and powerful serve. I was somewhat surprised yet delighted to learn only one other person, Jeff Hatfield, a long time member of the Wellington Club, served in similar fashion.

Although I continued to be involved on the Club committee, living permanently in my bach at *Pineglades* had its ups and downs with as many agendas among club members as there are months in the year. At that stage, I saw no reason to sell my house in Timaru, so I rented a flat in Christchurch. I still enjoyed dancing so Stanton suggested we join a square-dancing club. Luckily, I also found a new full-time position in the office of Beatrice Products Craft Wholesalers, located in Aranui. I was to continue working for this family-owned business for the next nine years. It was a completely different experience, living and working in the City, although I continued to spend most of my days off at the Club with friends and playing miniten.

Stanton and I at Foxton Beach shortly before we were married in 1989. Photo by Doug Ball.

Stanton and I began spending more than just time on the miniten court and square-dancing and before long I was sharing Stanton's home in Halswell. In February 1989 we were married in a quiet ceremony attended by just four other friends. I was now Kay Burrows. Reluctantly, I sold my home in Timaru, severing my financial ties, though not with family, in my home town. Stanton's house was also placed on the market, and together, we planned and built our home on a ten acre lifestyle block at West Melton, just ten minutes drive from *Pineglades*.

Hats are More Important than Pants

The roar of the frog-green T-bucket belied its sedate speed up to the clubhouse door at *Pineglades* on Christmas day, heralding my introduction to Flash, aka John Hart. It's hard to say who felt the most tension, me, when I saw my daughter in the passenger seat of said T-bucket, or Flash, when for the first time he met his future mother-in-law, who was wearing nothing but a smile, and of course her hat, while he kept his shades on.

During a conversation some years later, I learned from Flash he supposed I would put some clothes on to meet him for the first time. My response was pretty much the same as for any visitor to *Pineglades*. 'What's the point? Everyone else is naked!'

Jackie had met her Mr Right, but it would be another eighteen years and two gorgeous boys named Will and Hunter, before the pair eventually married in Timaru, after winning a wedding competition. Jackie achieved her dream wedding, all bells and whistles, and Flash got his piss-up and a barby, the following day. Until then, he was referred to as my very-nearly son-in-law.

These two absolutely dote on one another, with Jackie taking on motherhood with the resolve and capability similar to that of my own mother, who remained upbeat and positive in spite of her disability, and her authoritative and at times over-bearing, husband.

Building her own steady relationship, Jackie no longer commuted to Christchurch on a regular basis and sadly, no longer travelled with me on holiday. Even though Jackie had not lived with me for a number of years, I missed her terribly and still do. I greatly admire her as a person and never cease telling her I love her each time we communicate.

Unlike her own mother, Jackie prefers to keep her clothes on these days and Flash is more relaxed around naked people. For several years Will would spend a few days over the summer holidays with his Grandma and Granddad Brian, though less often as age and other interests prevailed.

Ever the organiser, in 1995 I found myself not only President of the Club, but also appointed co-ordinator of the *Mardi Gras Rally*. My 2i/c Tony Nee and his wife, Chris, headed a great team of people who all pulled in the same direction and ensured its success. On the night of the *Theatre Restaurant* held in the marquee, I looked in on these two gems in the clubhouse, as they were putting the finishing touches to over 300 meals, and considered myself fortunate to have these two as my good friends.

The week-long rally certainly put my organisational and motivational skills to the test. There were many other gems pulling their weight. Toilets, showers and marquee were cleaned and rubbish disposed of, lunches and beverages made available, entertainment both for the adults and youngsters provided, sports events organised and completed on time.

These rallies were very popular in the 1950's, in the days when there were far less ways in which to spend your leisure dollar, before television invaded our living rooms, and well before employment contracts were to impact on weekends and family holidays. I spared a thought for the guy who organised a rally at *Pineglades* several years before and which hosted almost a thousand keen naturists.

The New Year's Eve carnival party took on a decidedly Latin air, with one fruity bra ensemble an absolute knockout, several ruffled New Orleans party dresses and outstanding headgear added even more colour to the noisy carnival atmosphere.

As Rally Co-ordinator, I was juggling the myriad of responsibilities the event presented, which include NZNF Executive and Council meetings (what a hell of a time of the year to be sitting through an AGM), participating in sport and social activities as much as limited time allowed, as well as fronting up to the media.

A news crew from TV3 arrived on the grounds and during the course of our interview began quizzing me about the effects of melanoma. At that time a series of one day cricket games were being played.

I said, 'It always makes me wonder how cricketers who are out in strong sunlight, often without a hat for the best part of a whole day, seem to think a smear of zinc across their nose will ward off melanoma. Whereas we are far more nurturing and find shade during the hottest times, and wear a hat. I think hats are far more important than pants!'

For a number of years, I was known as 'Hats not pants Kay Burrows'. It follows that my 'Twitter' name is #hatsnotpants.

Hats are more Important than Pants

A glittering New Year's Eve party brought out all the Hollywood stars, and with big blonde wig, black stockings, and black and gold lame dress barely covering my derrière, I was a more than passable Dolly Parton, though others thought I was Marilyn Munroe.

Fizzing with our success on the sports courts, our contingent from Pineglades returned to the Mainland triumphant, suitcases bulging with silverware.

It was a fantastic feeling to have achieved success on the sports court, even more so in an environment that did not require clothing. I was convinced that skin is practical for any occasion, and those of us who enjoy our recreation without clothes, know that being naked is a great stress-buster.

Is that blonde dancing with June, Dolly Parton?

Look at animals for a moment. They get about in their birthday suits all day, every day. Just a minute, how come animals can get around with nothing on and the rest of us feel compelled to put some clothing on?

Animals don't feel the need to wear anything to attract other animals. But we humans go all out on that score, adorning ourselves with clothing to lure the attention of others, to conceal certain areas, or to draw attention to our breasts, hips, legs, or other parts of our anatomy as a fashion statement, to look sexy.

Uniforms are a universal component of the mix serving to identify a team, the service industry, health civil authority or those in the military. Henry David Thoreau once said, 'It is an interesting question how far people would retain their relative rank if they were divested of their clothes.'

In many parts of the world and depending on the culture in which you are brought up, you may find yourself wearing anything from a loin cloth to a hijab.

Until the arrival of Christian missionaries and Captain Cook in 1776, South Pacific Islanders wore little clothing or none at all. Not surprisingly, these primitive indigenous natives at first felt nothing but shame when forced to cover their nakedness.

For various reasons which were mostly brought about through being chiefly concerned with modesty and 'we have always done it this way', we humans have felt the compulsion to wear clothing. Okay, we want to be warm and comfortable. Certain types of clothing afford us protection from the elements when carrying out some occupations. Many psychologists say that the clothes we wear are an extension of ourselves, an expression of whom we are. But let's face it. There are times when clothing is just down right uncomfortable. Nudity, on the other hand, is often far more comfortable. In the garden, all kinds of sport, swimming, dancing, I'm not kidding here; just try it and see for yourself. Just generally, being out and about in the countryside when you feel like it. Surely it would be far better to divest yourself of clammy shirts and trousers, or bras and knickers and feel the sun and a breeze on your body, just as nature intended?

This clothes-compulsiveness locks us into a constant battle between individuality and conformity of dress. So, we are better off getting rid of this anxiety and enjoying the freedom of going without clothes. Who needs all the hassle of washing and ironing anyway? By not putting clothes on you give up all that social baggage, along with the nudity taboo.

You don't need to take a large suitcase with you on holiday either. All you really need is a hat.

Blast from the Past

Rather than become a 'pub bunny' in order to meet new friends, I completed the form for a dating agency based in Christchurch. *Contact* began well before the internet pervaded our lives. The forms were simple and the follow-up the same. Though 75 responses might seem somewhat daunting, I managed to cull 80% of them, which left me 15. Most of these lived in Christchurch and seemed to be worthwhile meeting for coffee and a chat.

One form that piqued my interest revealed that Brian, who lived in Timaru, owned a hobby house in Lake Tekapo, and was looking for someone who could handle a paint brush!

Mmm, there goes a challenge!

In an endeavour to find out a little bit more about Brian, I completely overlooked the fact he enjoyed country music; though many of his interests were similar to mine, it appeared he was fit and liked to go dancing and tramping. While I was pretty open about my own interests, it was difficult to expand on the subject of naturism by telephone, as opposed to a conversation in the flesh so to speak.

After several days of playing phone tag we finally connected and by then we knew each other's last names.

'Hello, it's Kay Hannam speaking, I have your name from *Contact*.'

'Yes, I know you. You used to live in Victoria Street and your father owned a taxi. You have an older brother called Rex.'

There was dead silence before I managed to collect my thoughts and responded, 'You must be Wayne Williams' brother? He was the same age and went to the same school as I did.' I'm thinking to myself, this guy must have gone to school with my brother. Talk about a blast from the past.

I was to learn that Brian had his own plumbing business in Lake Tekapo, albeit on a smaller scale than an earlier, similar venture in Timaru. Now semi-retired, he lived in a large home divided into flats, which housed employees in the township's burgeoning hospitality industry.

So, for the next couple of hours or so we reminisced about *Timaru Main School* and *Tech' College*, families and friends, our working lives and interests. And somewhere in the middle of all this, I'm sure I mentioned I spent most of my spare time at *Pineglades* and I liked to be au naturel. Our lively conversation concluded with a suggestion that if he wanted to see a bit more of me he should watch television the following evening, as TVOne was to present an interview between Jo Malcolm and me at *Pineglades* for the *Holmes Show*. The news doco' program was often controversial and enjoyed high ratings, so it was good publicity for *Pineglades*.

Unbeknown to me, Brian didn't have a television at Lake Tekapo where he was at the time. So he phoned an old girlfriend in Timaru, to tape it for him.

Before long, Judy was on the phone. 'You're just a grubby old man, Williams. All you wanted to do is watch the nudes'.

Brian was flabbergasted. 'What do you mean, nudes? I asked you to tape a program with Kay in it.'

He could sense Judy smiling. 'You don't know, do you? The interview was held at *Pineglades Naturist Club*. Everyone was playing volleyball and petanque in the nude!'

Brian by now was on full alert. 'Run that past me again?'

Understandably, the slant in our subsequent conversation began with, 'I didn't know you ran about without your clothes on.'

'Well, is that a problem?'

'No'.

Now we had that out of the way, it was time to meet. For me, I thought it would be the first time, because I didn't remember having met Brian before, even though he said he saw me with my sister Sue at a recent school reunion. We three girls were all quite young when Brian used to call around home to see big brother Rex. They were both involved with the *Rover Scouts* at the time and both would have avoided three much younger girls.

Our initial meeting in Christchurch's *Mona Vale* gardens meant a three hour drive from Lake Tekapo for Brian. Even though it was my day off, I was late and also forgot to bring the promised picnic lunch. Instead, Brian, armed with a hand-picked bunch of flowers, suggested we eat at a wonderful Italian restaurant. A leisurely afternoon followed as we viewed the number of colourful floral displays showcased by the city's *Festival of Flowers*. It was well after 10pm when, after a light meal and a few turns on the dance floor at a Hornby pub, we finally went our separate ways. I drove to my bach at *Pineglades* while Brian carried on down the main road and the long drive to Lake Tekapo.

Brian was to complete the round trip a few times before I finally introduced him to *Pineglades*. We had agreed to meet at the *Rolly Tavern*, about 2km from the club and on the main highway. The plan was to travel into Christchurch to *Sparks in the Park*, one of the mid-summer concerts held annually.

Wearing nothing but a sarong, I drove to the tavern and intentionally, or unintentionally, I explained I hadn't finished packing our picnic tea, and perhaps this would be a good opportunity to make a quick visit to my home away from home, before we drove into the city.

I knew as we drove down the long roadway surrounding the Club, Brian could see others through the trees, playing miniten and relaxing around the grounds. After parking alongside the bach, I walked in, nonchalantly untied my sarong and draped it over a chair. 'Okay, Brian, this is my home and this is how I am.'

Around midnight Brian telephoned after arriving back in Lake Tekapo, following the concert. He said to me, he nearly drove off the road laughing as he thought to himself, 'Williams, that's the first time you haven't had to try and get a girl's knickers off. She didn't have any on to start with!'

If I thought our relationship would blossom in the club environment, I was mistaken. As is typical of many failed relationships, there were those who tended to take sides, in spite of Stanton and Brian themselves becoming very good friends. I could only see further problems ahead and decided a smart move on my account would be to take a back seat, to be less involved with the club for the time being and develop other interests, now that I was a city-dweller. Sharing a home with my house-mate, Martin, also created another dynamic in my life and we had a great deal of fun.

Fortunately though, I only worked a four day week and it was inevitable that I would spend more time with Brian, at times exchanging my usual Thursday off with Friday and travelling south for a long weekend at Lake Tekapo. Passionate about naturism, my attitude was to try and establish a balance between our relationship and the lifestyle and recreational activities available at *Pineglades*. Before long we were involved in various social events again and making plans to travel to *Auckland Outdoor Naturist Club* and attend their *Medieval Rally*.

1997 was to be an even more eventful year. After having carried out an 'apprenticeship' during previous years as Trophy Secretary and South Island Vice President of the NZNF, the National President, Brent Thomson, determined I should be his successor. His were difficult shoes to fill, but his confidence in me was inspiring and when elected, I was determined to do my very best. During the opening ceremony I sat alongside Waitakere City Mayor, now Sir Bob Harvey, who is also patron of AONC. He's a likeable fellow and not at all fazed by addressing scores of naked people. I met him again several years later, only this time he was quick to exchange his Saturday 'corporate uniform' for a similar one to ours.

I have to say I was a bit miffed when I returned to work after our holiday. My boss said I should have consulted him before taking on this role. Perhaps he thought it would impact on my workload, so I was doubly sure that it didn't.

By this time we had introduced Martin to the love of his life, and it was now essential for me to find my own home, located in the city by necessity, rather than by choice.

Among the dozens of houses I viewed, one in particular seemed ideal for me, a stand alone town house located in a private back-section in Bassett Street. But as is often the case, this property was way beyond my price tag and so I continued to scour the real estate listings. The house was eventually taken off the market.

It wasn't until several weeks after initially viewing the house, that Brian, ever the problem solver, during one of his trips to visit, spotted what he thought would be a suitable home for me and viewed

Above: National President NZNF sitting alongside Waitakere City Mayor, Bob Harvey during the opening ceremony at the AONC Rally. Photo by Les Olsen; Below: Recognise him? Brian at AONC.

the property while I was at work. Wouldn't you know it was the same house with a slightly reduced sale price? While I was fairly relaxed about making an offer that suited my budget rather than the owner, it seemed everyone else was in a hurry. My instructions to the agent were not to bother returning, if the owner did not accept my offer. The sales agent, in training for a marathon, ran around to present the contract to the owner, whom I had figured was knee deep in debt building another house, then ran back to where I was patiently waiting, to complete the purchase.

Bassett Street met pretty much all of my requirements for city living. Easy walking/cycling distance to work and approximately 45 minutes walk into the CBD. My new house had enough storage space, but most of all, it was private and sunny, with an easily kept garden.

Although much of my spare time was involved with NZNF Executive affairs and Club activities, my life was busy and interesting. I enjoyed various art and personal development workshops, and joined the local table tennis club.

Brian and I enjoyed a family Christmas barbecue in my new home with Jackie and Flash, together with Brian's youngest son Jason, his wife Charlene, and their two young sons Andy and Sam. We then drove in Brian's Nissan truck all the way to Taranaki in the North Island, where we picked up what was to become known as *The Tardis*, a fibreglass camper which fitted on the deck of the truck.

After a brief stop at *Taranaki Naturists Club* we set off for *Rotota Sun Club* for their inaugural *Campout*, which was being held in lieu of the traditional sporting rally. My obligations as National President, again meant an arduous journey to arrive in time for the AGM three days after Christmas Day.

In spite of the long drive, *Rotota* was well worth the effort. With secluded, yet with expansive grounds set in bush on the shore of Lake Ohakuri, it is an idyllic retreat and though back to basics, *Rotota* offers excellent facilities.

A few weeks beforehand, a friend of mine and national PRO, Graham McGregor and I, had schemed to dress up as *The Topp Twins* and scheduled our arrival shortly after the AGM.

So there we were striding down *Sun Court*. *Camp Mother* beautifully made up, dressed in pink leisure pants with matching boob tube, complete with bandana, large beaded necklace and swinging a yellow handbag. *Camp Leader* appropriately attired in patterned full skirt, cardigan with stitched deer, green headband and back-pack full to the brim with tent and tennis racquet. *Camp Leader* even carried a fold up camp chair for *Camp Mother* to sit on later as she instructed *Camp Leader* in a loud bossy voice, to set up the tent.

Next minute we heard someone shout 'Oh look! There go *The Topp Twins*. TV3 must be here'.

Graham and I just looked at one another and burst out laughing. *Camp Mother* might have passed muster, but *Camp Leader* sported a full black beard!

Rotota not only put on the sunshine but also entertained us incredibly well, with a number of highlights during the campout, one of which was a magic visit to *Orakei Korako* geothermal area, *The Hidden Valley,* and possibly the best thermal area left in New Zealand.

Well known New Zealand naturist and photographer, Doug Ball, guided a large number of naked ramblers in awe of the gushing geysers and bubbling hot pools.

Climbing aboard a float plane to view the scenic landscape from above, earned another big tick from *Camp Mother*. Only this time I didn't have to wear a pink leisure suit. In fact I didn't wear anything at all.

Promoting with Passion

'What's so special about taking your clothes off?'

'It's not so much about taking them off, but not putting them on in the first place. I sleep in the nude, I get up in the nude, I shower in the nude and if it's a nice day, why bother putting anything on?'

Mike Hoskin, eyebrows arched and at odds with one another, vented a typical nasally-challenged response. 'Oh, I don't do any of those things.'

'What? Do you mean you shower in your pyjamas?' asked TVOne's *Breakfast* co-host, Susan Wood. 'I suppose you wear a pinstriped dressing gown, as well!'

Following the conclusion of the interview, NZNF Secretary, Peter Moosberger, in the Auckland studio during the link-up to the Christchurch studio, repeated Mike Hoskin's comment to me:

'She really is quite a nice person, isn't she?'

In response Peter had replied, 'Indeed, we are very lucky to have her as our National President'.

Being featured on *Breakfast* was quite a coup and the phone went red hot for some time afterwards.

In November 1997, my photo graced the front cover of the INF Bulletin. Its subsequent pages featured a lengthy interview with INF President Karl Dressen and went on to describe in great detail, my activities within the naturist community and my goals and aspirations for the NZNF. Understandably, I was delighted to be given such special treatment.

He also advised readers that I had received from Holland, the *International Naturist Information Centre* (INIC) Award 1997 *Woman of the Year*. Robbert Broekstra, INIC Director, noted in an accompanying letter, 'that every year if possible, the organisation names a woman and man of the year who have done a lot for naturism in his or her club or at national or international level. It was the first time that this award had gone to a president of a federation. Les Olsen, the first New Zealander to be honoured by the award, won it in 1996'.

Even though there was far more acceptance of nudism in general, the financial stress on younger potential members was also seen as a deterrent to joining a club and I believed a review of our traditional 'members' only', rule was relevant. Retention of existing members, coupled with an ongoing commitment to be an accepted part of the community, was also of prime importance.

Along with the Employment Contracts Act introduced in the early 1990's, the 40 hour week for many New Zealand families had disappeared and with that the freedom to enjoy club activities on a regular basis, as had previously been the case. It was acknowledged we were going through a period of change with many of our members ageing, resulting in a decline in the traditional voluntary aspects of maintaining club's facilities.

Several marketing ideas which my predecessor Brent Thomson initiated, included using the words *go natural*, accompanied by images of bare feet. Like all proposals for change this was met with mixed reviews, and while the words *go natural* were adopted, images of bare feet were not. Personally, I find bare feet one of the most innocuous of images and was quite dismayed to receive such negative feedback. The *go natural* logo was designed and used by the federation and clubs for many years, until later changed to *gonatural* under a comprehensive re-branding initiative.

The services and responsibilities of the federation were also under close scrutiny and at the 1996/97 Council meeting of the NZNF, the Executive was instructed to carry out an investigation into how the Federation was structured and the way in which it carried out its business. It was proposed that a full investigation be conducted by post, with the aim to get written input from every club member.

What this really meant was that the federation had agreed to conduct a national survey of members in an endeavour to gauge their views, such as whether the NZNF should set standards, membership security, ideas on membership retention, and how we described ourselves.

Of about 2000 survey forms distributed, 295 were completed and processed by NZNF Database Secretary, Peter Holt, with the actual comments of the respondents recorded on the database. From this database, Peter produced the 150 page *NZNF Survey 1998*, which gave an indication of the perception of the NZNF by members and club committees, its responsibilities and services, membership security and the INF Passport, retaining existing members, the structure of the federation, and how we describe ourselves and our activity. This informative document was given to federation officers and member club committees to use as a basis for future decision making.

A working analysis, or digest, of the survey results was also provided. This condensed version, accompanied by a separate, full list of all proposed NZNF options, was despatched to club committees, with a request to indicate which options they agreed with. These would then be formulated into proposals for the Council to consider.

The first of these were then put forward at the next Council meeting. One of these was the change of the name to *New Zealand Naturist Federation* to be used along with the term, clothes free recreation. The word nudist had long been determined as having a negative connotation, and it was agreed the word naturist better reflected the diversity of our lifestyle. Of course the immediate positive spinoff was the positive way in which we were able to communicate with the media.

Updating the old fashioned INF Passport with a new look NZNF membership card, and implementing a national database of members was quite a different matter. It was to take longer than my tenure as President for the Council to finally adopt this important step forward, with the central membership database accepted in December 2001. Although it took a further six or seven years for members to accept the recommendation to replace the outdated passport, it was satisfying to note that my original proposal for the new look membership card was, after a bit of tweaking, finally adopted.

Now the NZNF Membership Database is well managed by the NZNF and increasingly more understood by its members.

Many of my friends in the naturist community are of course, women and I have been fortunate to meet hundreds of exceptional people since I first climbed over the gate at Pineglades. June Campbell-Tong, herself a former national president and Jude Mercer, are two very good friends who work tirelessly in the interests of their club, Wellington Naturist Club, as well as the federation. When we met at annual rallies, we would often exchange and expand on ideas of how to attract more women, as we three knew of the wonderful benefits others like ourselves enjoyed.

Rather than lament there were far too many men, my focus was that there were not enough women. Several ideas for promoting our lifestyle to women were put forward for discussion. Women Only days, promoting our lifestyle at Women's Lifestyle Expos, with a nationwide promotion *gonatural* – It's a Woman's World.

The task of co-ordinating the promotion and getting clubs on board was taken up by the then National Secretary, Pam Kelly. A personal invitation was included for club members to present to their women friends, be they mothers, sisters, aunties, cousins, girlfriends, work colleagues, inviting them to take part in activities on a day set aside for women only.

Clothes free recreation was promoted as being a safe, leisure pastime for women and children. A place where we as women can feel comfortable and at ease, in spite of the less than perfect image some have of themselves. This was not about excluding men. It was about encouraging women to give them confidence, health and vitality and most of all, self esteem, in a supportive environment they would not find elsewhere. In spite of some sceptics, with some men literally digging their heels in, these ideas were well supported by clubs with many holding *Women Only* days on an annual basis.

Even if it rained all day and nobody turned up, the promotion was successful, follow-up from all the valuable free promotion being the key factor, which in turn prompted a rash of nude talk on talk-back shows and newspaper commentary.

While the northern hemisphere celebrated *World Naturist Day* at the beginning of June, for obvious reasons this was not practicable here in New Zealand. NZNF Public Relations Officer Chester Holmes suggested a *National Naturist Week*. In fact two were held, firstly a week in February following *Waitangi Weekend*, the other incorporating *Labour Weekend* in October. Activities reported, ranged from a golf challenge, a tug-of-war on the beach, petanque and volleyball tournaments with many clubs opening up their grounds to the local community.

Promoting and marketing the naturist lifestyle took on a completely new dimension with the introduction of the Internet which the NZNF embraced in 1998. The original website www.nznaturally.org.nz was eventually superseded by www.gonatural.co.nz under the new branding. This became the original portal for the NZNF, with information and links to all affiliated member clubs and resorts.

A few years later I was to feature in a book entitled *'With a Passion – The Extraordinary Passions of ordinary New Zealanders'*. A book that the authors wrote in their introduction: 'demanded a level of passion that was all-consuming and life-determining'. *'With a Passion'*, tells the story of 37 remarkable New Zealanders who are absolutely nuts about a cause, a calling or a collection, whatever the cost'.

Yes, I admit to being passionate about naturism and there has been a great personal cost but few regrets. I live the naturist life. I might not be naked all the time but if there's an opportunity to be nude when there's no real need for clothes, I make the most of it. Let's face it, clothes weren't manufactured on us, they were manufactured for us. It was only shame that made us put them on in the first place, as well as the desire to keep warm.

Creating the Place to Be

Brian says it went something like this . . . April 1998 near Lake Tekapo, we arrived at *Windy Ridges*, a property sandwiched between *The Wolds* and *Irishman Creek,* two 25,000 acre stations on State Highway 8, where he apparently had a plumbing job to carry out. In actual fact the job was at the house across the road.

There IS only one other house for miles and miles and it IS across the road. Both had been empty for some time. Rabbiters were long gone as were the rabbits, due to the Calicivirus disease illegally imported into New Zealand the previous year.

Keen to explore, I grab a hat – I'm wearing just sandals – and navigate my way down an overgrown track leading down to Irishman Creek, flowing along the boundary of the property, alone and at one with nature. Several million litres of water surge daily from the glaciers to The Wolds next door and disappear below ground. All that water?

I find a further track which takes me back to flat ground above. I don't have to look far to view mountains. They are all around me, the *Kirkalston Range* in one direction, *Two Thumb Range* in the other, the *Southern Alps* glistening on the north western corner with their majestic centrepiece *Aoraki Mount Cook*, its mantle of snow glistening in the sunlight.

By this time I'm glowing like the beautiful birches alongside the creek as I imagine quietly to myself, this rugged territory could be our new home, our new naturist homestay that is. I pick my way over the tussocks and rocks, avoiding the multiple varieties of animal manure. Brian is in the lounge making out he's attending to some problem with a fireplace.

'I quite like this place, in fact I could live here,' I enthuse. 'Okay, I saw the coal range and the pink cupboards in the kitchen.' Then I look to see what he is doing. 'Goodness! There's a hole where the grate should be.'

Brian calmly responds, 'Oh, they're putting in a log fire for us.'

'What do you mean, for US?' I retort.

With a deft stroke of cunning, Brian had arranged with *Environment Canterbury*, then owners of the old rabbit board property, that we would rent the house and grounds. In typical male fashion he had found a solution to the problem of where we could live in order for me to develop my vision.

Promoting naturism as an acceptable lifestyle choice was challenging within the confines of the Club. Understandably, everyone has different ideas. One of the main difficulties is that while naturists world-wide experience the benefits of health and wellbeing, many of them still keep it a secret. They keep it a secret from friends, family, neighbours and work colleagues. You would wonder why that is, when it is so good for you. It could be because of our Victorian upbringing, because of the perception the general public have of naturists, or the way in which the media often portrays anyone who simply enjoys being nude.

As one who has never been ashamed or embarrassed about my naturist lifestyle, I took every opportunity to speak with the media, write articles, and promote ourselves to the community in a creative way, including being guest speaker at service club dinners. A great way of promoting the club was to host the annual NZNF Rally. These rallies offer a valuable opportunity to talk about naturism and direct attention to the Club and its fabulous facilities.

Then the bombshell! Some months earlier the committee decided that *Pineglades* would not host the rally the following year as it had initially planned. Immediately I had a sense of déjà vu; years ago, I had had to advise the NZNF of a similar decision.

Of course Brian received my voluble reaction. 'I feel like organising the damn thing ourselves!' I ranted. 'We could form a steering group and apply for funding from community grants, the Lions Club and the local PTA to do the catering and cleaning. There are heaps of people around the country who would love to be involved in something like this.'

Over the years I had attended about fifteen national rallies and been part of well-run organising committees which cemented *Pineglades'* status as one of the top rally venues in New Zealand. Those of us who had participated in naturist rallies, or festivals, as they are now known, will have experienced a wonderful camaraderie, unique to naturist sports and social occasions. At the time, I was hugely disappointed the motivation was just not there. It looked as though the Manawatu Club would again earn the slot our club had abdicated.

Of the groups I joined since moving back into the city, the most inspiring was a network called *Successful Women*. A workshop I participated in was designed to assist successful women in *Naming, Claiming and Charging for it*. Within the first hour of this informative workshop, I had decided exactly what my ideal working environment would be: Outside, under the shade of birch trees, the sun's warmth dappled on my naked skin as I typed up an article or press release on my laptop. I wanted to form a business which would provide the opportunity to promote naturism; some form of naturist accommodation. A naturist homestay could become the catalyst in order for my vision to succeed.

At first Brian had rubbished my theory, but afterwards it became obvious he thought my idea had merit. Here, in the heart of the Mackenzie region, over which *Aoraki Mount Cook* presided majestically, was *Aoraki Naturally,* a naturist homestay that would become well known in naturist circles world wide. I would have everything except the laptop (which was to come later).

In very short order we both agreed *Windy Ridges*, with 18 acres of rugged farmland on a main tourist highway, would fit the bill. A suitable area at the rear of the house afforded sun and shade for a small number of campers, while many well established pine trees sheltered the property along sections of the boundaries, giving a lie to its name. The three bedroomed house seemed practical enough for bed & breakfast. Irishman Creek apparently never ran dry. What more did we need?

Timing was my problem. I was at the time, living and working in Christchurch, three hours drive north of Lake Tekapo where Brian resided. I really liked the prospect of living in Lake Tekapo and had made a number of new friends since we had first met.

I also planned to travel to Europe during the coming winter, taking in the International Naturist Federation World Congress in Sweden. Once it became clear that if I occupied myself with a marketing course at the local polytechnic before quitting my job and heading overseas, 'creating the place to be' could be a reality. I would be home in the spring.

If I thought my boss at Beatrice Products was happy to see me leave, then the smile on his face also told me he was genuinely pleased I was taking this big step into the commercial world. But there were a couple more details to complete, such as renting out the cabin at *Pineglades* and my home in Bassett Street. In very short order I found reliable tenants for both.

Brian was a bit cautious about letting the community know about our new venture. My response to his initial reluctance was, 'If we're not up front, then I'm not coming.' We need not have feared. Right from the outset, apart from initial larks in the pub, the small community of Lake Tekapo came to accept us wholeheartedly.

The following year was to be a steep learning curve. I enrolled for a government funded business course, and spent six weeks learning as much as I could about operating our own business, in order to qualify for a small business start-up grant. Seemingly, I passed with flying colours. However I was informed by the young desk-jockey from WINZ that due to the nature of my business, there would be no point in applying. 'We wouldn't want *Holmes* to know that we provide funds for a *nudist* business.'

I was incensed! 'If I am going to be discriminated against for operating a legitimate business, *Holmes* will hear of this.'

Arriving home, I gathered my thoughts and then telephoned him with a suggestion that I contact community and business leaders, in order for them to write letters in support of our venture. After telling me what a good idea it was, I then requested he put it in writing and fax it to me.

In pretty short order, I met the Mackenzie District Mayor, neighbours and business leaders, who all wrote glowing testimonials for me which I promptly despatched where required, with a copy to the regional manager. The application form was duly completed and the application process began.

However I was not out of the woods yet, as it took three attempts, in other words - three different panels - for my application to be approved.

The irony was that later I was invited to address similar workshops for would-be small business owners, on how to over-come obstacles.

Encouragement and support given by friends, neighbours, regional tourism, and local business colleagues during the following eight years, assisted me greatly in achieving my own personal goal that, 'naturism would become part of mainstream recreation'. Regional promotional material and books written especially about Lake Tekapo also now credit naturism as a valued part of the community.

We were grateful for the grant which went some way to fund the installation of powered campsites and the conversion of a number of corrugated iron buildings of varying sizes, beginning with the old chook house, which was converted into *The Perches*, with toilets, hot showers, kitchen etc. A large storeroom which had earlier housed poisoned rabbit bait and a large carrot muncher, was fenced in barbed wire and became *The Compound,* great for communal parties or relaxing around an acquired log-burner and by stacking firewood outside, our 100% recycled woodshed was transformed into a tidy en-suite cabin.

Clockwise from top right: Russell Giles tying the 'bridge' on Irishman Creek; The bridge builders: Gavin, Allan and Russell; Kay and Brian enjoy a quiet cuppa outside the 100% recycled woodshed - ensuite cabin; John Selwood arrives at *Aoraki Naturally* for the interview on TVOne's *Holmes Show;* Brian and Nud pose for the *Sunday Star*.

After an initial flurry of positive media attention which placed us on the front page of The Press, followed by an appearance on *Holmes* on TVOne, we were soon welcoming naturists and numerous first-timers, from all parts of New Zealand and overseas.

Many of these folk became firm friends, visiting and/or communicating on a regular basis. Several have contributed many hours renovating, painting, cleaning and clearing tracks, even building dams and bridges across the creek. To all these folk we are extremely grateful for giving up their own valuable leisure time, in order to help us provide this lifestyle for others to enjoy.

Positive media representation became the norm. Our scrapbooks bulged with newspaper cuttings, and we now had a small video library of television appearances. Even Nud, our Border Collie puppy, was featured together with Brian, in their birthday suits on Page 3 of the *Sunday Star*. 'Nud the dog is a natural'.

John Selwood, then a reporter from TVOne, contacted me with a request to feature our new venture on the *Holmes Show*, and arranged to bring a crew down after his trip to Antarctica. I thought to myself, at least he won't need so many clothes for this assignment. I duly organised a group of friends whom I knew would happily participate for the television feature. The resulting ten minute segment began with John arriving at our door, dressed in a smart suit, carrying a humungous suitcase. Later, he was captured strutting across the campground with his camp chair. He was the one who looked incongruous, but his intelligent questions and the equally intelligent answers from our guests portrayed *Aoraki Naturally* as an integral part of Mackenzie tourism.

While others would shy away from such exposure, for both of us, our enjoyment and immense satisfaction came from promoting the Mackenzie as more than just a beautiful place to stay. *Aoraki Naturally* had become the place to be, recognised world wide in naturist circles and admired for its rural simplicity.

From Casa Rosada to The White House

Twelve years since first boarding a flight to Europe, I was again on my way north, having agreed to attend the INF World Congress in Sweden, as NZNF Delegate.

Flying with *Aerolineas Argentinas* on the first part of our journey, Peter Moosberger and I stopped off for four days in Buenos Aires, the capital and largest city of Argentina. Walking this vibrant city revealed down-trodden areas contrasting sharply with ritzy neighbourhoods, mammoth trees, some reported to be over than 500 years old, heavy intricately carved wooden doors, thousands and thousands of gold painted taxis. Crossing 15 lanes of the main highway, we eventually arrived at the *Casa Rosada*, the *Presidential Pink Palace and Museum*, where Eva Peron would greet the masses.

Overseas travel can often be stressful and my arrival in Paris coincided with a severe stomach virus. My bags showed up five days later. Peter, who had moved on to London, allowed me to stay on in his sister-in-law's little flat where I drank nothing but herbal tea, venturing outside only briefly to explore the neighbourhood, before being reunited with my luggage.

Boarding the *Eurostar* bound for London and on to Bournemouth, I was to meet friends Roger and Vena Wright that same evening at 11:00pm, or so I thought. Due to a misunderstanding we met the following morning at 11:00am, together with Peter, also Bob Reed and his partner, Ron Wilkinson, who were both well known in Australian naturist circles.

So here I was, standing on *Bournemouth Railway Station* alone and it was almost midnight! I telephoned Craven Walker, owner of *Bournemouth District Outdoor Club*. Craven was quite a character. Luckily for me, Craven and his wife, Sue, had only just arrived home from a symphony orchestra performance, and he assured me he would pick me up in ten minutes. Sure enough, a snazzy red sports car arrived with this gregarious, elderly gentleman in the driving seat, beckoning his extremely grateful passenger to climb in.

No sooner had we arrived back at his home than he promptly opened a bottle of red wine to celebrate my arrival. I was to learn a great deal about this man during the course of a most entertaining evening, before he suggested I take the spare bedroom for the night. There was no question of floundering around in the dark looking for our chalet at the club next door, where our party met the following morning.

Though there were some similarities between BDOC and many other New Zealand clubs, it was obvious that this was where Craven had sunk a fair bit of his fortune. Chalets nestled among the gardens with a fabulous swimming pool, spa, sauna, recreation hall and restaurant, just some of the features at our disposal.

Before heading back to London we accepted an invitation to visit *Studland Beach* operated by *National Trust* and to have lunch. Who should be buzzing around in a light plane above, apparently taking photos of the naturist beach, was none other than Craven Walker. Then I learned something even more remarkable about Craven Walker. He invented the lava lamp!

Like many naturist beaches in the UK, *Studland Beach* has not been without controversy and is now restricted to a 1km stretch, which is still extremely popular.

Top to bottom: On Studland Beach. L-R Ron, Roger, Kay, Bob and Peter; Peter and Kay on Studland Beach; Outside Manor House Hotel owned by National Trust, L-R Bob, Vena, Ron, Roger, Kay, Julian Homer, Peter.

Once settled in to Roger and Vena's spacious Eltham home, we decided to visit one of the oldest naturist clubs in the UK, the following day. I had often heard my friend, Joyce Fleming, proudly relating the attributes of *The White House Club*. She had been a member of this established English club for a number of years before immigrating to New Zealand in the sixties.

Following a phone call to establish our credentials, the drive out was remarkably quick. However a couple of wrong turns saw us a little perplexed at first as to where the turn off was. This became all too clear on our return journey.

The White House Club, founded in 1933, is owned and run by the members and lies in the Caterham Valley, close to Caterham itself, approximately twelve miles south-east of London. As their brochure states, easily accessible by road, rail and bus. Junction 6 of the M25 is two miles distant.

Once inside the enclosed and terraced five acres of wooded grounds, we were able to join others at the pool side. But first, we were to disrobe in quaint and separate wooden changing sheds dating back to the early years of this club. Later, we were to find a quiet secluded corner under mature shrubs and trees, carefully planted to give protection and shade, as well as providing a screen from unwanted attention outside.

On the ground floor of the large and elegant home is the dining room, which has seating capacity for 40 members, lounge and fully stocked bar, members and staff kitchen. A lovely wide terrace to soak up the sun for after dinner drinks completes the indoor/outdoor social atmosphere.

Above: The White House Club swimming pool; Below: Roger explores the gardener's shed.

Tastefully decorated with good furniture and comfortable beds, the turn of the century three storied house boasts ten beautifully appointed bedrooms, the last of which was being decorated ready for guests, with sleeping arrangements designed for couples. Here was a peaceful haven for a weekend away to do whatever you do without the distraction of young children.

Having said that, I was informed *The White House Club* is a family club, similar to many of our clubs in New Zealand, where three generations of a family may be seen together. Their aim is to ensure an equal balance of gender to safeguard the spirit of naturism.

Like many of you who have travelled to naturist clubs, some form of water for splashing around in is essential. The 50' x 25' heated swimming pool is so deep at one end I lost sight of my friends. Luckily, the more conversational shallow end was half that depth and I enjoyed the company of members visiting for the day. Minimal chemicals are used to filter and purify and a cover ensures year-round use of this wonderful facility. The pool and surroundings would have to be one of the most picturesque I have ever enjoyed.

Completing the sports facilities is a children's pool, two tennis courts, table tennis, badminton, volleyball, petanque and billiards. If we had the time, I would have made the most of the Finnish sauna. That luxury will have to wait until next time.

After exploring the landscaped grounds with Roger and Vena, my pic' of the day would have to be the gardener's shed. *The White House Club* members, passionate about gardening, have all the tools for the job within this delightful amenity.

All too soon, the late afternoon sun's rays warm on our bodies, it was time to retrieve our belongings from the hangers in the changing rooms and go out into the bustle of the late afternoon traffic to find a nearby restaurant for tea.

My visit to *The White House Club* was a grand occasion.

Scandinavian Adventure

I enjoyed another good night's sleep before travelling to Gatwick for my next exciting journey – to Scandinavia. I had booked a cheap flight, and was looking forward to a few days looking around Oslo, which has a reputation of being very friendly and hospitable, but not this night. The sign at the airport said it all. 'No beds in Oslo'.

Now I found myself in a desperate situation and thought to myself, 'What would Brian do?' Brian would get on a train and go somewhere, which is exactly what I did, in the opposite direction to where I eventually wanted to be. It was so easy. Just get on a train, tuck my back-pack underneath me and sleep on the floor of the carriage, just like everyone else.

I woke up on the other side of Norway, in the coastal town of Stavanger.

Directed to a B&B by the station master, I slogged up the hill in the pouring rain, only to have the door slammed in my face by the owner, no doubt confused by my appearance and unmistakable non-European accent. Subsequent enquiries for accommodation around the village drew blanks, and after wandering aimlessly around this uninteresting port, I considered the best thing to do would be to board the train back again. This time I asked for an address in Tonsberg, Scandinavia's oldest town, approx 100km south of Oslo. I was bound to find accommodation there and I would enjoy sight-seeing on my way.

Following directions from the Stavanger Station-master, on arrival I boarded a bus to my destination which I understood was a couple of blocks away. Little did I know it would be almost 10:30pm when the driver, whose command of English was as abysmal as my knowledge of Norwegian, indicated our approach to what appeared to be a small hamlet. After ascertaining that the bus would return at 8:30am in the morning, about the same time as the train would be leaving, I managed to convince him to take me back to Tonsberg, where he deposited me at the bottom of a hill signposted YHA. Even before I got to the top of the hill I knew they would be closed. Sure enough the notice on the door said, Please do not ring the bell after 11:00pm.

Across the rooftops I could see a large sign, POLITI. Getting my bearings, I trudged across in the direction of the sign. Of course the door was locked, but through an intercom I managed to plead, 'My name is Kay Hannam, I am from New Zealand. Could I please come inside and be safe for a while?'

An encouraging click preceded a friendly voice asking me to come on in. To be honest, I can't ever recall being in a police station at any time, let alone on Saturday night after midnight in a brightly lit station in Norway. After listening sympathetically to my explanation, the duty sergeant asked me to take a seat, and endeavoured to find some budget accommodation for me.

My knitting was in the top of my pack and, clicking needles, I whiled away the next hour, entertained by all the drunks rolling in, with the added entertainment of a police psychiatrist interviewing those involved in domestic disputes. Eventually, the sergeant beckoned me over and asked me to complete a form.

I gave her a puzzled look, asking 'Are you going to put me in a cell?'

'You don't mind, do you?' she smiled.

'No, not at all, so long as you lock the door!'

Setting my camera on the edge of the stainless steel hand-basin I managed a quick photo which showed my glum face, before the lights went out.

Determined to get to Stockholm on the high speed train without any further hiccups, I scarpered out of the police station early the following morning with a quick thanks and reported on the platform well before departure time.

Locating back-packer accommodation in Stockholm was a breeze and I set about exploring this fascinating city. As is the case in many European cities, the architecture impressed me the most. Fortunately, I found the *Museum of Architecture*, with scale models of every significant building from the 19th Century on. I'm sure I recall scale replicas of other European cities as well.

The original ship of *Vasa*, after sailing just 1300 metres, sank on her maiden voyage in 1628, had been salvaged in the 1990s and now housed in its own special museum, visitors can crouch as they explore the ship. Swedish people must have been vertically challenged in those days. My sojourn in Stockholm culminated in an afternoon exploring an outdoor museum of colourful sculpture.

The sculpture garden in Stockholm.

Prior to leaving New Zealand, I had been in touch with Lola, who had directed me to a naturist campsite situated in the Stockholm Archipelago, which required a bus trip connecting with another, further out in the countryside, followed by a short trip by rowboat out to the island. There were four other people on the island including Lola, who then left on the return boat trip. Which left one other man, a semi-permanent resident, and a couple, the woman badly disfigured, whom I learnt had survived the Holocaust. They kept to themselves.

My cabin was the ultimate in minimalist Swedish design, but fine for my three day stay. Imagine my shock when at 6:00am next morning, I heard a loud blast on a ship's horn. It was one of the myriad of ferries plying the Archipelago; their corporate passengers enjoying a weekend excursion. I even spotted a yacht which had earlier participated in the *Round the World Race*. Other buildings on the island included a re-located schoolhouse which served as a club rooms, with a shop located near a children's playground. The short jetty built alongside the sauna facilitated a bracing cold plunge into the Baltic. Incredibly, every bit of wood and building material had been ferried across from the mainland. I recall the photo montage displayed in the clubhouse, which also showed a thick mantle of snow over the island in the wintertime. Sadly, this club which I imagine was worth several million Euros even then, is no longer a naturist club.

My cabin on the Stockholm archipelago

Eventually, I continued my journey south by train. Then, directed by a series of signposts to Galaxen, I eventually met Peter at the Congress venue. We both burst out laughing when shown to our hotel accommodation with its Super King-sized bed! Pulling back the bedspread revealed twin beds zipped together and we were both okay with that. It was at this same hotel I met the Canadian delegate and to this day, I continue to research this federation's informative magazine and website.

More than 20 delegates from as many countries were seated around the large oblong room, presided over by INF President, Karl Dressen, from Germany, flanked by various INF committee members, all participants with a dedicated microphone and earpiece. Three translators sat at the opposite end, listening and relating appropriately, French, German and English languages.

I wasn't here just to listen, and in typical fashion I took the opportunity to put forward my opinion on the ensuing debate. Before long I found myself at odds with the French delegate. After I pointed out that their proposal was unconstitutional, he animatedly instructed the meeting that the NZNF should be struck off! Thankfully the Dutch delegate, who had a better understanding of all three languages, was able to calm everyone down and a suitable amendment was put forward to appease both myself and the opposition.

Perhaps the most unexpected revelation during the weekend was that, although the Congress was held early September, everyone was fully dressed. Back home in New Zealand, unless the meeting is held during the winter or the weather is cold, we have a fairly relaxed dress code. I wasn't sure what to expect for the evening festivities which were very entertaining, but had packed something just in case. Everyone was done up to the nines.

However there were ample opportunities to get naked in the sauna and around the nearby lake, when we were not in the meeting hall. Scandinavians have a far more relaxed attitude to nudity compared to other countries, so I was very happy to be part of this community, if only for a short time.

Kay and Peter relaxing with friends in the sauna at Galaxen, Sweden.

Peter and I made our way south, towards Malmo, and again I was entranced by numerous beautiful sculptures adorning city gardens, many of them depicting nudity. A brief ferry and train journey saw us meet with another of Peter's sisters-in-law, who had found us a small back-packers hostel to stay in. Immediately she and I found a rapport when I learnt she was a dancer with the *Denmark Royal Ballet* company.

What to do in Copenhagen, one of the most liberal cities in Europe? An advertisement on a tourism brochure caught our eye, and we both agreed a visit to *Museum Erotica* would provide an interesting selection of art without inhibitions. Established nearly 30 years ago when Denmark first liberalised pornography, the first country in the world to do so, the museum is the oldest serious erotica museum in the world.

Amsterdam provided a homely B&B alongside one of the many tranquil canals, and we ventured south to Gouda and Delft, happily absorbing the wonderful culture of Holland before I departed from *Schiphol Airport* for another short stopover in Beunos Aires.

Not content with sitting around the airport for eight hours, I caught a bus into the city to further my exploration around *Puerto Madero*, which is now the trendiest neighbourhood in the city. At the time many of the old brick warehouses were being refurbished with the installation of a couple of interesting museums, one of which was devoted entirely to a display of plumbing merchandise. The other featured an incredible array of clocks.

Cripes! The time!

All that power-walking across *The Wolds* and *Irishman Creek* was put into good use. I arrived back to the central city, asked for assistance from a very helpful policeman, managed to catch a public bus, arriving back at the airport on the last shuttle, in the dark, just in the nick of time before catching the flight back to New Zealand.

Kay at Lake Alexandrina, near Lake Tekapo. 1998.

That First Step

Continuing my role as national president had its challenges, and living in Lake Tekapo meant communicating by email and a number of telephone conferences during the year. Interest was steadily increasing in naturism, with a steady surge of new members joining the federation.

Two years prior to our move to Lake Tekapo, Kevin and Joan Sampson overcame strong opposition from neighbours and created *Katikati Naturist Park*, with modern camping ground facilities and a number of chalets and deluxe cabins. Kevin and Joan set a high standard and after more than ten years developing the park, were rewarded with the New Zealand Tourism Industry Award for Best Holiday Park and were in the final top three two years later.

Winning a mainstream tourism award caught the electronic Media's attention in a positive way and the Park received worldwide publicity. This has had benefits not just for their business but also for naturism generally, particularly in New Zealand.

During the next few years I continued to learn new ideas, attending a number of small business workshops in the South Canterbury area, in particular those which offered marketing advice. *Aoraki Naturally* joined a proliferation of naturist home stays, eventually called the *Naturist Homestay Network*, which then affiliated to the NZNF. The network, which grew to fourteen in a short space of time worked well, forwarding referrals and exchanging promotional material, not only with each other but with other clubs as well. But, there was an element of distrust among some in the organisation, worried that the increase of commercial naturist venues would soon overtake the club model, undermining the naturist federation of members.

Nothing could be further from the truth, as the increasing number of visitors would often take that first step at a privately owned venue, where there was no compulsion to join, or be part of a committee or working-bee.

Many of these visitors, having satisfied their curiosity, would broaden their experience by contacting a club at a later date, to arrange a visit and eventually become valued members.

I was advised of a course in web design which was being held in Christchurch. So off I went every Wednesday afternoon for the next six weeks to learn as much as I could about the *World Wide Web*. This was 1999, in the very early days of the internet, and, while the federation and many clubs had a presence on the 'net, I knew very little myself. Luckily, I secured the domain name www.naturist.co.nz, and before long I had MS Front Page conquered. We had our own website! Not only did I set up pages of relevant information about *Aoraki Naturally*; after taking on the role of Co-ordinator of the *Naturist Homestay Network*, I compiled listings for several of these and ensured that the network was represented with their own dedicated web page.

This also led to my next initiative: to update the defunct *Taranaki Naturists Club Camping Directory* which had lain dormant for many years and create *Holidays NZnaturally*, a guide to clothes free holiday destinations in New Zealand. With the approval of the executive, I set about compiling the guide on MS Publisher, with each venue's location and contact details set out in a similar format to those of other regular camping guides. Both North and South Island maps formed the basis of a regional index.

One of the obstacles I needed to overcome was the secrecy in which many naturist clubs veiled the location of their venue. I figured the best way was to just go ahead and provide as much contact information as I could find, with a street address and a map directing visitors to their destination. Nowadays, the internet provides a wide range of options which makes life far easier for everyone, especially the visitor.

Holidays NZnaturally worked well and included a wide range of naturist venues, with both affiliated member clubs of the NZNF and those who were offering accommodation, preferring to share their own naturist lifestyle with like-minded visitors. It provided an easy reference for visiting naturists, many of whom were from overseas, for accommodation, clubs, home-stays and resorts and, thanks to *Free Beaches NZ*, a list of the more popular naturist beaches.

Some years later, I introduced an electronic version of the guide. Both are updated regularly, and offered on our website. If clubs in particular, retained the same domain name, telephone number and email address, not only would it save a great deal of time and energy updating this information, but they themselves would be found far more readily by prospective members or visitors.

That First Step

In the early years I sold a considerable number of guides, but the introduction of another publication reduced the demand. I still get a great deal of satisfaction refreshing the content each year and of course finding an interesting cover photo. Many happy recipients refer to the guide as 'the little gem' and upon arrival, perhaps two or three years after purchasing it, tell me they use it as an integral resource for planning their naturist holiday in New Zealand. The guide is ideal for those who want to find out a little more about naturism, or are just plain curious. And let's face it, most people are not really comfortable about their own nudity, but are incredibly curious about others!

I agree it takes a little bit of courage. For many, the fear of being nude in a public setting rivals only that of the fear of public speaking. I've done both and thankfully, I have never forgotten my own initial experiences of social nudity. It's one thing to swim without clothes in your own backyard pool. But quite another matter when there are other people around, especially when they are mixed sex.

While it's true that men often initiate visiting a naturist club or resort, it is clear that with just the simple act of divesting their clothes, couples tend to feel more comfortable with each other. Rather than detracting from the intimacy they experience with their partner, their relationship with one another is strengthened. Couples who spend quality time together in a secure and congenial environment, free from perverts and other unsavoury characters, feel less inhibited towards each another, particularly those in a new relationship. Simply by feeling better about themselves and each other, naturists experience a healthier sexuality.

Steve and Glen 'global naturists' from the UK, in the chilly waters of Irishman Creek.

The first time I was naked in a social situation, I felt empowered and really good as a woman. I certainly didn't think it was a brazen thing to do. Many women in particular, seem to think they have to overcome the idea there are so many things that may be wrong with them. You think you're different to everybody else. But it's not until you look in a mirror and think, 'well, this is what they'll see, this is what they'll get. It's no big deal, so if I can handle it, why can't they? It is then that you realise you're no different at all.'

There are so many pressures on women from magazines and the fashion industry, with countless advertisements suggesting you should be slim or shapely, you've got to have great abs or boobs, a good butt or whatever. Once you get past that and you feel good about yourself, that's half the battle of being nude in a social sense.

I consider myself average weight, height, whatever, but quite frankly I don't really care whether I am or not. Even at the age of 66, I just think I'm OK. I have never had any problems seeing my own nudity in the mirror, but a great deal of women do.

Those who come to visit us, come from all walks of life. People in the legal profession, even a couple of High Court judges, not together, you understand, though it wouldn't matter if they did, doctors and nursing staff, IT specialists, musicians, a significant number of current and former air force personnel, care-givers and teachers, including those who teach children with special needs, farmers, business people, some from the real-estate industry, and even other holiday park owners. Quite a few of our visitors are retired. Few, if any, are unemployed, while many are English or European.

Their nakedness is the only commonality naturists have but it's amazing how when you are in the spa, or swimming pool, or just having a meal together, it tends to even things out. One evening I would be chatting with a retired bank manager and alongside me there may be a dairy farmer and his wife. It really wouldn't matter. There's a level there, they find. I can't explain it. Maybe it's the nakedness that does it.

In my experience, being able to leave your cares behind with your clothes when you check in at a naturist resort, opens up a whole new way of making friends.

Countless people have told me how they have taken a holiday together at an ordinary holiday park and in an effort to make new friends have never gone further than 'Hello, what's your name' or 'Where are you from'. Now, having spent time in a naturist environment, visitors say it's like a wall has come down. They have made so many new friends from all over the world and wonder why it took them so long. I heard someone say, 'You meet the nicest people when you're nude'.

My greatest reward has been seeing other women bloom. The first year we were at Aoraki, a woman named Janet came to stay. Janet worked at a hostel down south; her friend, from the North Island, was meeting her at the *Lake Pukaki* lookout. Janet was a bit younger than me and had what you might call a fuller figure. Her friend was a bit of a hard-case and had arranged the weekend visit, but conveniently forgot to mention where he was planning to take her. I don't know who was more nervous upon their arrival, me or Janet.

But I do remember we were cooking dinner together in the kitchen on the Saturday evening. It was getting pretty warm and Janet, who had earlier in the day gone topless, suggested we should have a nude dinner.

'That's a great idea,' I agreed, then cranked up the old coal range a bit more. When her partner arrived back inside with Brian, they were both gob-smacked by the two of us standing at the sink, peeling potatoes with not a stitch on.

At Janet's request, Brian took some great photographs of her among the colourful lupins growing prolifically around the Mackenzie region during the summer. She wrote and told me she displayed a couple of the photos in her room, so her other girlfriends could see them.

Talk about the first step! Janet covered miles in self-esteem during her first weekend at *Aoraki Naturally*.

Nude with Attitude

The Blue Dome of Freedom at Sweetwaters

Sweetwaters Festival revelled in the heady, freedom loving traditions of other musical festivals in the 60's and 70's such as *Woodstock* and closer to home, at *Nambassa*. Many of those attending indulged in a unique atmosphere which captured the essence of clothes-free attitudes.

The last *Sweetwaters* was held 15 years earlier, and this one, planned for the end of January 1999, was held on the Puhinui Reserve, near the Auckland airport at Manukau and promoted as a huge community event, which reflected the diversity of our collective creative expression.

It was to be more than just a music festival, and provided us with an ideal platform to share information about clothes-free recreation, the wide benefits of living the naturist lifestyle, free beaches, clubs, resorts and home-stays.

That less than 20,000 people, rather than the predicted 50,000, paid an admission fee, is now history and attributed to financial disaster for the organisers and some of the promoters.

The concept of *The Dome of Clothes Free Recreation* was visualised by Aucklander, Tony Judson. Keen to bring together groups and promote the naturist lifestyle, Tony's first approach to me was to gauge the NZNF Executive's thinking. The bit was firmly between his teeth.

Sending out information to clubs and organisations within the federation was the easy part. The lack of response from some quarters was frustrating. However, success was measured by the reaction of visitors to our display site and from the very first day we set up our display, the word was out about the blue dome.

For reasons beyond our control and understanding, the organisers had decided, just days before the festival began, that *Sweetwaters* was to be promoted as a *family* event and there would be NO Nudity! Quite counter-culture to previous music festivals. However, not wishing to get offside, we carried on in our own space, as we had received nothing in writing and placed a sign outside 'If nudity offends, please do not enter'. That got their attention!

Our display proved to be a real haven for thousands of young people, and not so young, keen to find out about the *Blue Dome*, which stood out among the myriad of tents and displays like a beacon. A couple of young artists added a floral touch to the already bright exterior. Inside, it was hot and humid and our team were kept busy fielding inquiries. A massage booth was curtained off and many took advantage of this service.

Delia Adams from Auckland arrived with bundles of *NZ Naturist* magazines and to help set up display material provided from clubs and field enquiries. Arriving at the shower block, at the end of a long day preparing the site, the two of us could not believe our eyes when we saw dozens of people using the outdoor showers, completely clothed.

Top: Outside the Blue Dome at Sweetwaters; Bottom: Visitors lathering up with free sunscreen inside the dome.

I was keen to be as free as possible and wore a sarong when enjoying the opportunity to visit one of the five music stages. Incidentally, the main stage had 96 speakers! Even for this slightly hearing impaired music lover I thought it was a bit extreme, my only experience of a music festival being the *Edinburgh Tattoo*.

But I digress, back to my preferred Jazz, Blues and Roots Stage, where I was relishing the atmosphere and music one afternoon. It wasn't long before I was approached by a couple of police officers, and requested to put my top on. A smiling police constable informed me that people would complain if I didn't. My response was that their action was merely trying to precipitate a complaint. Only half an hour before, I had walked right in front of one of their top brass who didn't raise so much as an eyebrow.

I point blankly refused to cover up and told them my nipples were no more offensive than those of the man sitting alongside wearing shorts, nor the lesbian dance group performing the previous evening, wearing skirts only.

What was interesting was the amount of support around the venue from complete strangers, who told me later they would have removed their tops if I had been arrested. The police presence was quite intimidating and prevented a lot of women from going top free which was a great pity, as their action would certainly have changed the situation. In and around our campsite, we remained nude although the police compound was only a couple of hundred yards away. Talk about inconsistent!

Tony's original idea was to award clothes free enthusiasts around the festival site with bottles of sunscreen. The no nudity policy prevented this idea. Instead he and Chester Holmes from Wellington, used their upper torsos as a living signboard, with body paint advertising *'Free Sun Block'*. The sight of Tony in his baggy shorts and bright yellow sun hat daubing sun block on all and sundry, created quite a stir around the stages in the hot Auckland sun.

The response, 'You're a lifesaver. Sit down and have a beer with me, mate, you're doing a great job'.

This gave a strong message that naturists are concerned about skin cancer and we also care about people. Supplies were quickly depleted, as thousands responded to the invitation to come to the *Blue Dome* and slap on some more free samples.

A woman came in and asked us to look after her bags while she carried out another message. Several were spotted walking around reading *NZ Naturist* magazines. By Sunday, we estimated around 70% to 80% of those who had visited *Sweetwaters*, knew about the *Blue Dome*.

Sure, we had the gigglers and radio jockeys who could not differentiate between lewd and nude. This was countered positively by a number of television interviews from local film crews and the opportunity for our team of assistants to be clothes free, with some of our visitors choosing to shed their clothes while inside.

We agreed with Tony that this promotion, without a doubt, helped lift the image of organised naturism in New Zealand, to those persons present. If clubs in New Zealand so happened to field a few more inquiries than usual, then they might have thought about the half dozen or so people who worked their bare butts off in *The Dome Home of Clothes Free Recreation* at *Sweetwaters*.

Kay along the bank of the Tekapo River. 1999

Nude Zealand – Nationwide

The catchy melody of *The Pink Panther* set the scene for a revealing *Inside New Zealand* documentary on naturism, screened nationwide in 1999, on TV3. Having been involved with much of the research with the producers, *Ninox Films*, I was eagerly anticipating *Nude Zealand*.

A grin spread over my face as the camera panned over a group of naturists from *Nelson Sun Club* gathered around the piano, enjoying this lively prelude. Not the usual plate of sandwiches at ridiculous angles in the name of modesty for this prime time screening, nor were we subjected to any pixelated penises.

We were expecting this, but were the rest of New Zealand?

More happy people enjoying a barbecue in the sunshine at the *Wellington Sun Club* and my buddy Ken Mercer morphing from clothed to naked, gave way to a view of the *Rolleston Fire Service* driving into *Pineglades Naturist Club*, for the annual *Waitangi Day* volleyball tournament.

Getting to Know You, a timeless signature tune, provided harmony for the warm-up games and frank commentary from the neighbourhood, a happy meld of families at ease with each other, as they have been for the previous 16 years of the competition. The burning question, 'do you get your clothes off?' was answered with a well-timed cue into the crowded swimming pool, by a larger than life fire officer, lifting his hat in salute.

Retired bank officer, Geoff Fenn, told how he'd traded in his business suit for his birthday suit. Geoff and Wendy, who look upon themselves as *Global Naturists*, graphically presented the benefits of visiting naturist venues in their motor home, cycling through the glade of trees at *Pineglades*, followed by the exhilarating hot stream at *Rotota*.

Four generations of Colin and Daphne King's family, bear witness to this lively couple, and now we all know Colin's first foray into Nudism was at *Waitaki Boys High*, in the 1930's, where the Principal made the kids swim in the nude.

'It was compulsory and what's more,' said Colin, 'a genuine nudist never wears anything to bed'.

Kathy Trott of *Mapua Leisure Park*, recounted the stiff opposition from Nelson churches to their popular clothes optional beach resort, where at that time more than half the annual 2000 holiday-makers chose to go nude. A young couple acknowledged their own conservatism was a good reason to come to *Mapua*, and gave their children a nice balance.

The year before, a Nelson newspaper again drew controversy, with a front-page photograph of three naked women frolicking across the grounds at the *Nelson Sun Club*. The board member of the *Baptist Church* was asked during the documentary, to state his case.

'In any society where there is an absence of clearly defined moral guidelines, then women will be the victims of a moral decline, not the perpetrators and therefore women in particular, ought to be concerned about a society in which a moral decline is being promoted or advocated.'

A further question, 'The nudists we've met seem pretty harmless, so why do you think nudity is indicative of a moral decline?'

His answer: 'I guess I really don't know, but I think it is.'

Bringing nudism to the conservative town of Lake Tekapo did not prove to be such a hurdle for Brian and me at *Aoraki Naturally*. Max Bygrave's warbling rendition of *I Love to Go a Wandering*, provided another humorous touch as we were captured on film, setting out for an afternoon stroll, with the Southern Alps in the background.

Here, the acceptance of our naturist homestay by the local community was apparent when filmed during a neighbourhood barbecue. My daughter, Jackie, was also on hand to express her enjoyment of growing up in the naturist world, yet like so many young women, susceptible to other influences in her life.

A further interview followed with two young teenage girls, both third generation members at *Pineglades*, who expressed their difficulty in being unable to accept the natural changes in their bodies, as their parents had. The documentary lacked a balance of opinion from youth at ease with nudity, particularly in front of their peers. Yes, I know they are a little thin on the ground, but they are there.

Unfairly, in my view, single men came in for their share of attention, with a cautionary tale from a club official, stating they liked to retain a balance of male and female.

'Thankfully,' she reassured us, 'only on one occasion they were required to ask a person to leave, because of his inability to control.'

Social nudity ended Brent Thomson's sexual confusion we were told and after spending some time on beaches, we learnt he joined *Auckland Outdoor Health Club,* now *Auckland Outdoor Naturist Club* (AONC), at the age of 19. Now, years later enjoying club life, his view of club members is that they are nice people. He also pointed out, that 'there is a big difference between guys who are a little enthusiastic on their first visit and others who go around creating problems for others.'

When Delia Adams found naturism, she also found the courage to face her demons and started to heal from a traumatic childhood, finding openness and a way of getting rid of all her inhibitions. She sent a strong message to women that they need to be at ease with their body. It's a barrier that women need to come to terms with.

There were many other interviews and like these, identified the full name of each person. This informative documentary which enjoyed a repeat screening later in the year, was natural and of tremendous educational value, dispelling many viewers' preconceptions.

'If I had problems, I'd definitely go to a nudist camp, because they seem like such caring, warm people who help you through anything.'

'I thought nudism was all about sex, but there's nothing sexual about any of it.'

'What an amazing feeling that'd be, walking through the bush, nude. I'd like to try it.'

'How refreshing to see normal bodies on TV. I felt a lot better about myself after watching it.'

Typically, a feature of this nature drew a great deal of controversy, but it gave me tremendous satisfaction to read the following item in the *NZ Herald* on 29th September 1999.

'Scenes of bare breasts and male genitals in a documentary about nudists did not breach broadcasting standards,' says the *Broadcasting Standards Authority.*

The *Inside New Zealand Documentary, Nude Zealand,* shown on TV3 in June, prompted Aucklander Kristian Hatrang, who had never seen male genitals on television before, to complain to the authority.

He said the documentary portrayed nudity as normal, whereas few people in New Zealand were nudist and many would object to nudity being screened in their homes.

He also objected to the 8:30pm screening time, saying it could have a detrimental effect on children and young people.

However, TV3 said the show's depiction of nudity was innocent and non-sexual and portrayed the nudists' bodies matter-of-factly. TV3 said verbal and written warnings preceded the show and it was shown at an adult's only time.

The authority refused to uphold the complaint as the footage was 'entirely relevant' to the documentary and did not breach accepted norms of decency and taste. The use of warnings and the screening time did not breach broadcasting codes regarding children and viewing.

The Beginning of an Endless Summer

Brian and I had travelled up to Christchurch to meet friends at *Pineglades* and to play some miniten before the winter set in.

Relaxing later in the clubhouse, I spotted a beautifully illustrated brochure pinned to the notice board. 'At the foot of the old Provençal village Reillanne, between Forcalquier and Apt, lies hidden in a beautiful valley, at an altitude of 350 metres, the naturist paradise *Le Vallon des Oiseaux* (translated in English), *The Valley of the Birds.*

The colourful brochure went on to describe the 50 hectare site, which apparently enjoyed a Mediterranean Sea climate, with more than 300 sunny days per year!

Checking out the visitors' book, we noted the entry dated the previous day, 'Jan and Madeleine Pasma, with Amanda and Roman, *Le Vallon des Oiseaux*, France.' If only we had been here a couple of days earlier. They only stayed one night, in the cabin alongside the one which used to be mine.

I said to Brian, 'I'm really sorry I missed them. If ever we go to France, I'd like to visit their lovely campsite and meet them all'. Little did I know this was to happen sooner, rather than later and our endless summer would begin.

Although Brian was conditioned to severe winters experienced during the years he and his family spent in Lake Tekapo, I was not and barely ventured outside, even though I wore several layers of clothing. With a metre of snow piled up outside the door; stoically fuelling the coal range and log burner was not my idea of fun. I was used to warmer climes and less clothing!

Brian and I celebrate our first and last winter together.

But I was willing to try. After all I was living in what was purported to be a winter playground. My early years as a child, ice-skating at Lake Tekapo, held me in good stead and I managed a few passable figure skating moves, but try as I might, I never got past the learners' slopes on *Round Hill Ski-field.* I would continually crash into a bank, prop myself up and start all over again, while Brian would careen fearlessly down the face.

Surprisingly, it was the sport of curling where I was able to unleash my competitive spirit and did fairly well on the rinks.

Roads in the Mackenzie were hazardous in the winter, with tourists gazing in awe as *Aoraki/Mount Cook* unexpectedly came into view on their left. The immediate effect would be the car doing 'the 100 yard dash' and flipping upside down in the ditch on the opposite side of the road. Every now and then we would hear a loud bang emanating from the road below our house, as a car would slip on the shady ice patch through *Irishman Creek Bridge,* then take out a section of our neighbours' fence.

Even though I was a bit blasé about travelling, the opportunity to attend as NZNF Delegate to the *INF World Congress* in Germany presented itself in 2000, coinciding with the *World Expo* in Hanover. After having sampled naturism in the northern hemisphere, there was more to learn and plenty to see and do, plus I could write about my experiences. What's more, Brian and I planned to be away during the worst of the winter.

There's always something special about roaming the streets of Paris. Again, as was the case two years before, it was clean-up time after *Bastille Day* celebrations. I pictured myself among the thousands lining the *Champs de Ellyses* as we walked over to the *Eiffel Tower*, deciding against joining the hour-long queue and opting instead for the more modern form of seeing the panorama of famous landmarks from the *Millennium Ferris Wheel.* We were pleased we had spent most of our day soaking up the rich atmosphere of the *Notre Dame*, and the artists' quarter along the banks of the River Seine. No queue at the *Louvre* however. It was Tuesday and closed for the day.

Two days later, we were racing along the A1 in a brand new Peugeot in search of *Athena*. It was well after normal reception time when we finally drove through the gate, to find hundreds of cars parked under the trees.

Hey! These Belgians must have had a party going on. Reality dawned later when we were provided with a little hand-cart to take our belongings to our campsite beyond the rather large clubhouse and office.

A trip across the border the following day to the neighbouring village of Ossendrecht, allowed us to appreciate the countryside and admire the creative way Dutch people care for their homes and gardens. *Athena* was well signposted – at least from this particular direction. We were eager to return to soak up some sunshine and explore the spacious grounds, which offered many opportunities for members and visitors to relax in this privately owned resort.

We spent two days luxuriating in the pool and wandering around wooded campsites; the sun filtering through the numerous lime trees onto the Petanque piste and volleyball courts.

It was our intention to visit Amsterdam and we satisfied ourselves with a short tour, courtesy of new friends from *Chamavi* near Almere. Holland is full of interesting engineering achievements with windmills, canals and dykes which provided fascinating fodder for us both.

Then back to *Chamavi*, where our friends were rostered on for cleaning duties in the large clubhouse. The previous evening we had shown videos of the Mackenzie and Canterbury regions in New Zealand, also a special screening of the television documentary *Nude Zealand*. Club members were surprised to learn of the number of naturist sites in our country.

Keen to sample the hospitality of others, we readily accepted former INF President Bart Wijnberg's invitation to stay with him and his lovely wife, Wads, in The Hague.

It's always fun to take holiday snaps and the stairs servicing no less than five floors in this 17th century home, placed a new angle on Brian's nude photography. Double doors opened onto a lovely, secluded garden, planted with a variety of trees and shrubs. In the hallway, a portrait by Inge van den Thillart, provided a stunning backdrop for our host, who was also a regular contributor to the Dutch naturist magazine, *Naturisme*.

A short bus ride with Bart the following day led to the beach for a swim in the North Sea. An interesting visit to *Maduradam*, on the way back, gave us further photo opportunities of this beautifully scaled model miniature town, which included a naturist beach.

There was more excitement in store; this time on the A10, which thankfully, we left at Hoorne. *De Vrije Vogels* was easy to find and after pitching our tent in a nice sunny spot, we went in search of company. We were finally getting a grip on the handcart idea, even though it meant our little alpine tent was full to the gunnels. Although the caretakers, Wilma and Piet, our immediate neighbours, were very friendly, Brian's challenge to a game of darts was met with rather a brusque response from the heavy smokers in the clubhouse.

We appreciated the loan of our neighbours' table and chairs the next day and enjoyed a relaxed, albeit late, breakfast under the trees in this former fruit orchard.

An early start meant we were well down the A7 heading for the longest dyke, to Leeuwarden. Finding *Kuinderloo* was a bonus. Heavy rain and no visitor accommodation determined a quick tour around lush grounds instead, campsites screened for privacy – I can't think of any other reason. In spite of this it looked a lovely place to stay, with a good swimming pool, separate youth hall and . . . No smoking!

When one thinks of the reclamation of land in the Netherlands, it comes as no surprise to occasionally find a small but deep lake in the middle of club grounds, with its own sandy beach. One of these is at *Osana*, near Enschede, where we were greeted by the lovely Annie, a naturist of 35 years, caretaker for 14 of them, in this relaxed style of club terrain.

Pitching the tent just before another shower of rain, we were grateful to be given free rein in the beautiful club house kitchen, complete with fridge, washing machine and dryer. This was more like it.

Several of the 400 members contributed to the construction of the Clubhouse, which had a lovely, open feel about it, with heated tiled flooring. It sported 9 clean showers and toilets and a large tub for washing very young children. There were about 25 youngsters on the grounds for the holidays, obviously enjoying themselves, all day and every day.

A visit to the *Old Mill* at Humeill which dates back to 1188, gave us our first experience of the German countryside. Topping up with veges in the huge supermarket complex on the border, we returned in time for a game of Petanque on one of the two pistes made of crushed brick.

Osana sat well with us and our stay capped off an enriching experience in Holland.

The *INF World Congress* took place the following week at the naturist site of the club *BffL Hanover*, in Misburg. Hosted by the German Naturist Federation, representatives from 24 different federations were represented.

Guests were accommodated in rented caravans, well equipped with bed linen and towels and supplied with electricity. We were provided with superb buffet meals during the Congress.

Retiring President, Karl Dressen, was in his element chairing the proceedings. But the most interesting speaker was Ulrich Reinhardt, who gave a detailed lecture revealing the latest tests on the leisure-time behaviour of young people.

Karl Dressen completed 22 years of involvement with the INF and was nominated Honorary President. Improved and open communication during previous years, both with INF officials and other federations, assisted tremendously in establishing our credibility at this Congress. The genuine friendship of INF members was clearly evident, as was the sincere appreciation for the NZNF contribution.

Taking a bus into the city to view the *World Expo* seemed the most sensible option, as parking would be a problem. Finding our way was certainly another! Just as well both Brian and I are relatively fit. With mouths agape at the tremendous variety of exhibitions, we walked solid for the next eight hours, absorbing as many impressions as we could without actually travelling to each country. But there was one part of the world we wanted to explore further, France and *Le Vallon des Oiseaux*.

Nude with Attitude

A Taste of Europe

The President of the French Naturist Federation or Federation Francaise de Naturisme (FFN), Philippe Cardin, directed us to the region of Alsace, where we felt the warmth of the French people. It was a pleasure to visit *Centre Gymnique d'Alsace* near Wassalone, where we met FFN Department President, Charles Obergfell, and his wife, Marlene, who invited us to their home. Perfectly ripened melon, a vessel for a shot of port wine provided a mouth-watering starter for a luncheon of true French cuisine.

Some privately owned sites allowed club members to implement their own social program, and by paying an annual fee enjoyed a year round campsite, without the day to day responsibilities. One of these was *Gremoin Nature*, in the Rhone Valley near Vienne, where we revelled in the company of owner Robert, club members and visitors from Holland, around the barbecue one Saturday evening. We were greeted by yet another warm welcome from the Club President, Luc Mereau, who presented me with a club cap and a bottle of the local producers wine.

As we travelled further south, we joined thousands of holidaymakers from the north at a number of privately owned naturist campsites. Facilities were first class, with restaurants, luxurious swimming pools, cafe bars and a wide range of accommodation options.

Earlier in the day, I had telephoned *Le Vallon des Oiseaux* in Provence, where Dutch owner, Jan Pasma, and his wife, Madelaine, established themselves in 1987. I politely explained I was Kay Hannam, from New Zealand, and that Brian and I would like to come and visit *Le Vallon* for a couple of days.

'I know you, I know you!' came Jan's excited and unexpected response.

'Why didn't you tell me you were coming? I would have had some accommodation for you. It is the high season!'

I quietly explained we had a small tent and would take up very little space, which seemed to pacify him, but he was anxious to ensure we knew the way. After assuring him we did, I hung up and related to Brian what had transpired on the telephone. Now armed with the bulky, yet necessary Michelen map book, our arrival was timed for shortly after 4pm, mindful of the fact it is generally accepted that visitors do not arrive at European naturist campsites during 'siesta'. We would be in time to set up camp and have a swim before cooking dinner.

After parking the car in the designated car park, we easily found the reception area and offered our INF cards to Madeleine as the normal guarantee of stay. 'Non, non… you are the President,' she quietly remonstrated before handing back our cards, offering us instead a welcome drink and more apologies for not having accommodation, 'but Jan would invite you for dinner at 7 o'clock.'

And with that, we were driven up the hill in a golf-cart to a beautiful campsite looking over the valley where we set up our tent in among the pine trees, alongside one of the two swimming pools and next to two friendly Dutch people, Bab and Liesbeth.

Meeting Jan was like being greeted as a couple of old friends on the crowded terrasse. None of this 'table for two' lark, and room was quickly found for us at a noisy table full of Dutch people. Effusive introductions all round included daughter Amanda, who, 'will take you horse-riding tomorrow,' and, 'Thjys will escort you on a tour of Provence on Thursday'. Saturday apparently was party night with entertainment and 'a big buffet'.

All our objections, 'we only planned on staying a couple of days,' fell on deaf ears to the amusement of our new Dutch friends.

So we allowed ourselves the time to explore the lavender clad hillsides, old abbeys and quaint neighbouring towns. A leisurely ride on their beautiful Friesan horses around the 130 acre property with Amanda, was one of the many highlights.

We were the butt of jokes, as Jan noted in his daily newsletter. 'The Kiwis are going horse-riding, and if they fall off, please to help them back up.' But it was the circuit at breakneck speed in Jan's 4WD which resulted in an adrenalin rush. Mad as a hatter, but great company.

We did manage a spare evening and accepted a warm invitation from a young Italian couple camping down the hill from us. It was our first taste of real home made pasta, albeit cooked over a campfire. As with many of the friendships we formed in Europe, we were to meet Salvatore and Anna again and continue our friendship until this day.

It was in the swimming pool I was 'at peace' and swam several lengths each day, before stretching out in the warm Provence sunshine with a book. As was expected, Saturday night's buffet provided masses of food and wine, with regular entertainment a hit with visitors crowded at tables alongside the pool. Even Jan joined the band with what became evident, a repetitive rendition of Frank Sinatra's *My Way*.

The hundred or so visitors had a great time and we all very much enjoyed this type of outdoors meal, but it was obvious to both of us it was a lot of work for Jan and the family.

Those of you who know Brian, will agree he is a workaholic and one of these people who just can't help himself. Before long he was in amongst it, clearing tables, rinsing plates and cutlery.

He asked Jan, 'Why don't you get more staff to help you around the camp?'

But all Jan could say was, 'I can get good textile staff, but I would rather have naturists to work for me'.

'Well, we will come back next year and help you,' offered big-mouth Brian.

Jan thought he was joking.

Poker-faced, Brian replied, 'No, I would not joke'.

'We will talk about it when we come to New Zealand again, next year' said Jan.

Five days at *Le Vallon* were balmy, but fun and we certainly revelled in the equally hilarious farewell as Jan, ever the entertainer, brought out a cornet from his collection of brass instruments and gave a rousing rendition of *Colonel Bogie*.

We went in search of *Mas de Las Balma* in the Languedoc and were rewarded with one of the most natural naturist sites we have seen. Yet again, as the first New Zealanders ever to visit, notwithstanding a visit from the NZNF President, we were considered 'exceptional' by the young receptionist and led to a wonderful shady site, a short walk from the river below. We were pretty self-sufficient, but their little shop had plenty of provisions in case we ran out.

Our timing was perfect, as the traditional *Cargolada* was planned for the following day. We eagerly snapped up two of the remaining places and looked forward to spending five days in this beautiful Catalonian region.

Seated by 12:30pm under a canopy of colourful umbrellas, we eagerly consumed the starter of barbecued escargots, accompanied by the first of many pichets of red wine. While the meal itself was delicious, even more exciting was seeing the chef, resplendent in red and white costume, sprinkling salt, pepper and chilli powder (which had the effect of knocking them out) over hundreds of live snails, before grilling them on a very large open barbecue on the ground, full of glowing embers. Our hosts delighted in informing us, a consumption of 80 to 100 snails per person would not be exceptional, especially for those who love this dish.

Large bowls of salad and fresh bread accompanied grilled Catalan sausage, not your usual sausage, formed neatly into regular sized offerings. Instead, this large circular sausage was barbecued whole, with another wire grill on top in order to turn it over. It was a simple matter of snipping off as much as you wanted to eat.

But wait… there was more, in the form of large pieces of spicy barbecued chicken, before we lumbered down the bank for a welcome siesta, only to be advised that we were expected to assemble again at 8:30pm for more festivities and even more food. This time there would be dessert as well.

I was to learn our host, Geans Borratt, was overheard rehearsing a speech in English while taking a shower. Imagine my delight when during the lengthy *Cargolada Part II*, he rose, and welcomed the President of the New Zealand Naturist Federation to *Mas de la Balma*.

With a grateful 'Merci', I presented him with a copy of our *NZ Naturist* magazine.

Later in the evening I had consumed sufficient red wine to convince me I should sing *Pokarekare Ana* just for good measure. Although the words were unmistakably Maori, it was probably just as well he didn't know it was a New Zealand love song.

Further exploration led us to a festival at Arles Sur Tech, situated in a valley separating France from Spain, and an ancient Catalan tradition called *Castells*. The trick is to build a human pyramid, and dismantle it by climbing down. Teams trained weekly and were dressed in traditional coloured team shirt, and white trousers, with a wide black scarf wrapped around their torsos to support their backs. No ropes or helmets, just sheer determination and guts!

Sweltering in the hot Catalan region, we headed south into Spain, with place names and directions in both languages; the distinctive red and yellow striped flag banned in Franco years, fluttering prolifically at every balcony and masthead.

Barcelona's architecture has always fascinated me, so the invitation from the President of the Spanish Naturist Federation to meet and have lunch, was accepted with alacrity!

By studious reference to map references, and keeping calm in frantic traffic, we duly arrived at our meeting point in a parking building in the city, a safe place to leave the car and meet our hosts, waiting outside a large department store below. It was a short drive before being escorted up several flights of stairs to their apartment overlooking the city, and while discussing naturist beaches in the region over tapas, we had a bird's eye view of a rooftop soccer field. In the distance were the golden towers of *La Sagrada Familia*. I have to admit they looked more beautiful from a distance, than up close.

Nearby we found a whole shop full of witches and chose a beautiful craggy specimen to add to my small collection back home. Clutching bags tightly, we explored side streets before a quick guided tour by car around the impressive *Olympic Stadium*.

It was time to hit the beach!

It was a little over an hour's drive from Barcelona is *El Templo del Sol*, a magnificent location adjacent to *El Torn* beach where nudity is mandatory. Noting the railway line running parallel to the 1700 metre beach front, we chose a campsite that would give us the least disturbance during the night, then explored this well equipped resort.

In addition to a 300 seat movie theatre, the bar and Jacuzzi which seats around thirty people, overlooks the swimming pool. In fact there are three cascading pools, over a surface of 1300 m2.

If only we had a few weeks, not a few days. There was more to see and do and on our way back we stopped at *Figueres*, withstood the hour long queue, and toured the *Dali Museum*. Surreal!

Choosing the fast motorway route we eventually found the *Club du Soleil* in Paris, tucked away in a back street. Our first impressions of the facilities noted these were fairly primitive by today's standards. Perhaps it was under a historic buildings covenant. The building itself was an old abbey with a small area of grass at a higher level suitable for camping, though vehicle access seemed non-existent. A small block of apartments constructed in stone, housed our overnight accommodation. Yet another apartment was used semi-permanently by Christiane Lecocq, widow of Albert Lecocq, founder of the FFN in 1950.

We were to meet this sprightly nonagenarian the following morning. One of her grandchildren had driven her from *Monte Livet*, the site where the INF was first founded in 1953.

This was our first taste of Europe together. We knew with certainty it would not be the last.

Nude with Attitude

Sunhats and Shoes . . . Only

Of course the reasons for holding a naturist festival at *Aoraki Naturally* were obvious, with many of those planning on attending the *NZNF Rally* at *Pineglades* also indicating a desire to visit us as well. It was also a great way to promote clothes free recreation as a mainstream activity in the beautiful Mackenzie region where we live, and a terrific opportunity to open up a naturist event to the public.

This was new territory!

But, I had visions of blocked toilets and cold showers, resulting in 30 or 40 disgruntled visitors, instead of the usual handful our homestay would normally accommodate.

'Let's organise something,' said she, with the mouth as big as the wide-mouthed frog.

Brian - the list from last year almost complete - gave a knowing smile, mentally extended his use-by date, and immediately began renovating the chook-house to accommodate campers' kitchen, showers and toilets. *The Perches* was soon a reality and proved quite a conversation piece.

As the months went by it was likened to holding a tiger by the tail, such was the interest by the media to this rather extraordinary event. The first ever, national bare buns fun run and nude golf tournament on a registered golf course, were great fodder for an eager news media.

Encouraged and supported by both Canterbury and Mackenzie Marketing groups and the local community, I sent out an initial press release in June. All the major newspapers responded and reported the details. By the time I was ready to send the next in November, a sharp Sally Rae from the *Otago Daily Times* arrived, camera in hand, for the first of many interviews. The result was front page coverage in major newspapers and several broadcasts on radio.

Planned for 5th – 8th January 2001, following the *Pineglades Rally*, it was evident the muster would attract around 50 to 60 visitors (we would eventually top 90). After checking the bylaws and discussions with the *Mackenzie District Council*, marquee and portaloos were ordered, extra vans borrowed/hired, registration forms sent out and entertainment and catering delegated. In fact the whole nine yards normally orchestrated by a committee of a dozen or more. Brian and I used to joke about having a committee of three: Me, him and me.

I designed a commemorative logo with the outline of a naked kid and footprints leading to an outline of Aoraki/Mount Cook. *Mackenzie Muster Naturist Festival* took on a ragged font similar to run holder information, stamped in black on a wool bale. Tee shirts emblazoned with the logo and the date also had the words *I saw you naked in the Mackenzie* and our website www.naturist.co.nz scribed on the back.

Stuart Croft owned a sound and music business in Timaru and he and I planned the cross-country course together. Among many day to day activities, he also supervised the fun run, lawn-mowing race, Highland games (a sort of Scottish Top Town), as well as the sound system. Stu also provided us with a magnificent trophy made out of Macrocarpa and rock from (oops, I am sworn to secrecy) to be presented to the winner of the 7.5 kilometre fun run.

Brian and I had earlier applied to a national body for funding to assist with promoting the event, as we knew this would capture the imagination of the media and give naturism in New Zealand an extremely high profile. We were pretty devastated to learn not only would we be no longer entitled to assistance, but they had been informed (incorrectly), the funding would be used for prizes. The person responsible for pulling the rug out from under our feet was well known to us and considered to be a friend!

Anthony Bailey, from the *Lake Tekapo Hotel*, came to the rescue and thanks to his valuable assistance, we managed to keep our heads above the water line, instead of drowning completely.

Mike and Jill from Wellington had visited us the previous winter, and vowed to return and look after everything while we attended the rally at *Pineglades*. These two gems crossed off items on 'the list' with great gusto and stayed until after the Muster was finished, working practically non-stop during their holiday.

I don't know who had the best time, us or daughter Jackie and her pal Wendy. These babes were the 'toilet toilers'. They arrived for the weekend, pitched their tent and pitched in, yellow gloves and all. Not just content with cleaning toilets and showers, they were willing helpers at all times and everyone enjoyed their company. Our heartfelt thanks went to these two wonderful girls and to the many other visitors who arrived and crossed off items on the list.

Any apprehension established naturists may have felt towards opening an event to the public was quickly dispelled, as several naturists from the UK, Canada, Holland and Australia joined their New Zealand counterparts for the *Gathering of the Clans*, in the marquee on the Friday night.

In an endeavour to give *The Address to the Haggis* a truly Scottish flavour, we had written to *Wilson's Whiskey*, of Dunedin, with a request for banners and a dram or two of their golden nectar to accompany this treat. We were surprised when a courier arrived with a case of 1150ml and a case of 750ml bottles and the banners as well. Needless to say the whiskey loving musterers consumed more than just a dram or two during the evening. We were entertained by Allan and Raewyn Campbell on bagpipes and keyboard, with Allan providing a stirring rendition of Burns' ode.

Murray Mackay can always be relied upon to get the crowd going, and true to form, kicked off the rest of the evening's entertainment. The matronly crew of *Dot's Lot* had the crowd in fits later, with their hilarious take on the *Blues Brothers*.

Members of the *Lake Tekapo Lions Club* were enthusiastic with their support and practical help, providing a barbecue meal for nearly a hundred people on Saturday evening, plus a buffet meal after Sunday's golf tournament. Proceeds were given to the *South Canterbury Hospice*. As well, a large number of Timaru and Lake Tekapo businesses offered sponsorship for the weekend event.

Although sunhats and shoes were 'de rigueur' for most competitors, the lure of being able to run (or walk) unfettered, saw most competitors baring almost all around the curvaceous course on Saturday. All that freedom of running through

Top: Members of the Lake Tekapo Lions Club serving up the barbecue – and not a tie in sight!
Bottom: The inaugural Mackenzie Bares cross-country fun run.

the wide open spaces was pretty exhilarating. Something our overseas participants were especially taken with.

A young Canadian won the women's cross-country event. Cheryl was on her first visit to New Zealand with husband Ron and had been a naturist for 20 years, but never before run in the nude. It was a fun experience for her, running through the undulating tussock-covered farmland and negotiating the chilly creek, with the mountains in the distance. 'The whole event has been awesome,' she said.

Cheryl's prize was a scenic flight for two, which she and her husband took the following morning. The scenery confirmed her hopes to be able to come back to defend her title.

The men's race was won by Les Rootsey, editor of *The Australian Naturist* magazine (TAN), and the walking section was won by Graham Macgregor of Tauranga. Two special prizes were awarded to; husband-and-wife walkers Stan and Barbara Gartner of Hamilton who celebrated their 44th anniversary on the day and to Donald Washbourne of Christchurch, who, at 76, was the oldest participant.

First up after lunch was the *Great Nude Zealand Lawn-mowing Race* and *Highland Games* including tossing the mallet and warratah throwing (extra care being necessary here for both onlookers and participants), along with what could have been the world's first ever dog trial event which used nude humans as both sheep and dogs.

The Great Nude Zealand Lawn-mowing Race gets underway. Mackenzie Muster 2001.

Dress code for the *Tartan Tie and Boot Party* was adopted in many ways by party-goers, with one sporting his op-shop purchase. 'It's an optional kilt, depending on how you wear it,' he said, as he adjusted the size 8 kilt on his adult body.

A stage had been set up at one end of the marquee. Once the last crumb had been devoured and the Lions club members had cleared Sunday evening's fantastic repast, we settled back to watch *The Clan Concert*. Talk about the good, the bad and the outright diabolical!

The Canadians stole the show with their enactment of *The Cremation of Sam McGee*. There were four Canadians altogether: The youthful Cheryl and Ron, and the older, Cliff and Carol. Ron, as narrator, took the stage at right, seated at a table. Cheryl appeared, pushing a wheelbarrow carrying Cliff, aka Sam McGee, and climbed on to stage left with Carol, who was wearing a full length fur coat - from Brian's shed?

As Cheryl gripped the wheelbarrow handles, Carol slipped off her fur coat, revealing a full body harness on her pale body. Now please don't tell me they found this harness in Brian's shed as well!

The crowd was in hysterics as Cheryl whipped her 'husky', by now on all fours pulling the wheelbarrow/sled, as Ron solemnly read the ode. She reached the table/furnace and tipped Cliff/Sam in. Ron, nearing the end of the ode, peeked in the furnace as Sam croaked the last few lines.

'Please close that door. It's fine in here, but I greatly fear you'll let in the cold and storm – Since I left Plumtree, down in Tennessee, it's the first time I've been warm.'

Not everyone was happy about the naked event in their midst and we learnt that an anonymous person wrote to the editor to express their extreme displeasure. However, because the person had not signed the letter, the newspaper would not print it. Instead, the editor showed it to Lake Tekapo Community Board Chairman, Bruce Scott, also a member of the *Lake Tekapo Lions Club*, involved in setting up the marquee and catering for the festival, and who was reported in *The Timaru Herald* saying, 'Tekapo has been given a huge promotional boost because of the *Mackenzie Muster Naturist Festival*.'

The following letter was published a week later.

'Naturist gathering'

'My wife and I have just witnessed an extraordinary event and we would like to pass on our experience to readers.

We were visiting from Australia to participate in the inaugural *Mackenzie Muster*. This was a four-day weekend of fun sports events in a Scottish theme, held at *Aoraki Naturally*, a naturist (yes that is a nudist) homestay near Lake Tekapo.

The event was excellent and a huge success, as we expected, enjoyed by near 100 persons from infant to ancient from North and South Islands, Australia, Canada and Holland.

However, the part that made it extraordinary was the fabulous attitude of the local people. Nudist events are so often the subject of apathy, misunderstanding and/or ignorance.

This one was totally backed by the Lake Tekapo and Mount Cook commercial interests – sponsorship for sport prizes was accumulated to the tune of several thousand dollars in the form of tourist product discounts, fixed wing and helicopter flights, accommodation, even a sampling of the local tipple. Extraordinary.

However, it gets better. The local Lions Club (clothed) produced a fabulous barbecue to get the show started and an afternoon buffet style dinner on final presentation day. The *Balmoral Golf Club* allowed exclusive use for perhaps the first ever, 18 holes in the buff, on a public golf course.

Well done, Lake Tekapo and Mount Cook. Their attitude is exemplary and welcomed in the naturist movement. Their generosity will be repaid.

The event has already been the subject of much welcome press, both here and abroad, and its success will mean an inevitable repeat, perhaps annually and a 'must-do', in many naturists' activity calendars.

Australia could well heed the Mackenzie's generous open-minded example.

B N McDonald
Northern Territory, Australia'

Needless to say, there were many more favourable news items following the event. A couple of weeks later I received an envelope containing a newspaper cutting from *The Independent*, published in London, with a photo identifying the *New Zealand's Bare Buns* event at Lake Tekapo, together with a note from one of my old work colleagues in Christchurch.

'I can't go anywhere in the world without seeing a photo of Kay Hannam's bum'.

leg of our journey before arriving in the walled city of the *Palais de Papes*, Avignon. It was only a short walk to the tourism centre to find a hotel for a few days, before meeting Suzanne and Bernard.

By this time I had had my fill of cities and textile living and eagerly accepted their invitation to stay at *La Sabliere,* a naturist centre on the Ceze River. Our *Oliver* mobil-home, set among well-established oak and lime trees, blended easily and quietly into the natural surroundings.

We have always liked dining out – in France especially – and the restaurant at *La Sabliere* produced an extensive menu. The shop below afforded a variety of goods and fresh fruit & vegetables.

Huge chasms naturally carved out of the rocks had nicknames such as *The Arches* and *The Gendarmes.* Every camping site was within easy access of sun or shade, and most areas had power, water and drainage. The banks of the Ceze were covered in fine stones and coarse sand, with the river very deep in parts and quite wide. Steep in places, the service roads around the 50 hectare site were all sealed.

We swam in one of the two large pools which had a huge glass cover that slides back during the warmer months. A more energetic two hours were spent on the fitness trail, thankfully shaded by oaks, chestnuts and lime trees. *La Sabliere* has numerous activities and workshops during high season. Aqua gym, hiking, yoga, pottery, ceramics are some as well as a varied children's program.

Bernard and I enrolled in the art class which was held under the plane trees. This would be my first ever attempt at drawing a nude model and I soon had a handle on line and form. With practice I could only get better.

Better still, was the VIP reception at *Belezy* in Provence. The Manager, Pascal Leclere, had arranged for a basket of flowers and local products in addition to the usual bottle of wine to be left in our chalet to welcome us. We were to meet this charismatic young man later for a drink in the large restaurant and bar.

Brian persuaded Suzanne it would be a great idea if he and Bernard checked out the car rally being held in the nearby village of Bedoin. As well as the more up-market *Eden* bunglow in which we were to stay as their guests, there were *Cabanon* bunglows as well as cabins and mobil-homes which had basic comforts, including wc and shower. Numerous camping pitches in the woods were sited among natural hedges and flowering rock planters.

'Give your body a holiday,' was the advice from Jacques, whom we met at the Hydrotherapy Centre. We could choose from a wide range of therapies, from steam bath to massage. Oh, to stay two or three days and not just one!

I settled for a dip in the ultra large swimming pool before dinner in the crowded indoor/outdoor restaurant which had a live band playing. With only a few more hours until we would begin the next stage of our journey, Brian and I made the most of the opportunity to dance the night away.

As we travelled along the familiar tree-lined N100, I reflected on our visit twelve months earlier, following the *INF World Congress* in Hanover. We had enjoyed five days camping at *Le Vallon des Oiseaux* and became firm friends with Dutch owner, Jan Pasma. Brian had jokingly offered to lend a hand to finish the toilet block, only to be taken seriously.

Jan's visit to New Zealand helped to seal the deal, and now we were back for ten weeks to help around the campsite in return for accommodation, meals and a healthy allowance of red wine.

The daily grind for Brian at least, began at 7am, cleaning the 18 x 10 metre swimming pool. A few short horn blasts heralded the arrival of the bread van, which he and Fred, one of the regular Dutch campers, unloaded. The first of several coffee breaks followed before checking the water supply, then down to the stables to feed out the magnificent Fries trekking horses.

I would give a cheery wave to Brian, back in the kitchen by this time and seriously into food preparation. With fresh produce grown in the huge vegetable garden there was plenty to choose from. Meanwhile I would be on my way to check my emails after completing 50 or 60 lengths of the sparkling pool. Temperatures were minus ten at Lake Tekapo. I decided the best I could do here was to have a leisurely breakfast in the shade. By 10 am it would be around 35 degrees at *Le Vallon.*

Afternoon siesta sat well with me. I either slept in our tree-shaded caravan or snoozed alongside the pool before reporting for duty at 4pm in reception. Twenty years ago, working as a barmaid at the *Crown Hotel* in Timaru, I would have been chastised severely for pouring a beer with a head of two and a half centimetres, but that's the way they like it in Europe!

My lack of French, or Dutch for that matter, rarely became a problem. Puzzled looks transformed into smiles when patrons realised we were Kiwis. Happy hour turned to a frenzy as pizzas and frites were despatched by the French cook, Patricia, followed by a lull before Jan, attired in white apron and not much else, gave the first cry of 'Potage!'

By week four, the swimming pool kiosk had opened. Posters and maps from *100% PureNZ* and Mount Cook/Mackenzie adorned the windows of the now *Kiwi Bar*. It was to get even busier. Happy hour was now on the terrasse overlooking the pool where Jan would often organise a buffet meal for over 100 guests, entertained by *Tinkers,* an Irish band from Avignon.

Le Vallon des Oiseaux, a 50 hectare naturist centre in a beautiful valley tucked away in a lovely part of Provence, is renowned for its lavender fields. The centre is nestled below Reillane, a picturesque village some 80km east of Avignon between Apt and Forcalquier in the *Parc du Luberon*. Half an hour's walk would find us in the centre ville for the Sunday market.

Bastille Day celebrations meant fireworks displays, top bands and dancing in the village. This was to be repeated a month later, only the fireworks were set to classical music in this centuries old village. A little like *Sparks in the Park* on a smaller scale, but with an incredible 12th Century backdrop.

Each week we visited colourful markets in nearby villages and immersed ourselves in the history and atmosphere of the South of France, including Sisteron and the famous Citadel, renovated no less than seventeen times.

A breathtaking view high above the beautiful harbour of Marseilles followed a cruise from the fishing village of Cassis, sweltering in the *Canyon de Colorado*, (no prizes for guessing what colour this was). An exploration of the *Gorges du Gorge* with its 1,000 metre cliffs was a breathtaking challenge, taking all day to walk 14kms in temperatures of around 40 degrees; trundling along in a little train to Nice, the pace of which reminded me of the old rail car in New Zealand, passing through 52 tunnels sometimes at an average speed of 65kph, we spent an afternoon at the Mediterranean Just for good measure, we visited Avignon again during a musical festival and quaint little cafes at every opportunity, to savour the food of Provence.

By the end of August, most of the Dutch holiday makers had returned to Holland. It was the turn of the French to go on holiday. Numerous dinner parties during the week signalled our own final farewell from Jan before boarding the high speed TGV Train à Grande Vitesse (French high speed train).

Less than three hours later, we were window shopping and gazing in awe at the architecture of Paris, already planning our return to France again the following winter.

No sooner were we back home, getting stuck into all the spring cleaning and welcoming our first visitors for the summer, when in November – one of the most exciting times in my family's life – Jackie gave birth to a son, Will Henry Hart. To be with Jackie and Flash during this very special moment and cutting the umbilical cord was an incredibly emotional experience for me, and one that I will always be grateful for.

I was now *Grandma*, though for a long time afterwards, Flash would call me *Nana Nud*!

Animals, Dead Ants and Dog-wallopers

Not much grew in the Mackenzie during the cold winter months. We could expect daffodils and irises in the spring and in spite of the barren surroundings, rhubarb and potatoes would continue to flourish in the chicky poo patch. Our merinos were secure in their paddock with the occasional check by a neighbour to ensure their well-being.

Ebony and Ivory, two wild cats Brian had acquired some years before, were on holiday at a Timaru cattery; no doubt dreaming of all the wild mice and tasty baby rabbits (immune to the Calicivirus) that were fattening up nicely for their return to the wild.

Nud was being cared for by Rex Miles, one of our neighbours. Incidentally, Nud was only five weeks old when he curled up in my lap for his very first ride in Brian's truck from Burkes Pass. His mother, also a purebred Border Collie, had nine puppies, all of them male. As their owner required only seven for training, two were to be put down. Personally, I think they got it wrong as Nud is the most intelligent, loyal and obedient dog and fun to be with. Nud is introduced to our guests as the Entertainment Manager.

Although the Mackenzie was a natural playground for Nud, *Irishman Creek* was where he was in his element. The trick was to throw a stick upstream. Nud would wait on the other side, before bounding into the fast flowing creek to secure the stick before it disappeared out of his reach, then swim across to deposit it at your feet, before swimming back to the other side to wait patiently for you to throw it again. Nud never tired of this game, but others did.

We often watched campers relaxing with a book. Nud would bring a stick or a tennis ball and drop it at their feet. Inevitably, after several quiet steps forward with various missiles, our guest would put their book down and the aforementioned missile would be projected as far away as possible, only for the whole process to repeat itself. Several times visitors have said to me, they have tried to ignore him, but we know it is an automatic process whereby your arm has a mind of its own – or Nud's.

Then of course there was soccer. Thinking it was a sheep, he naturally barked at it while playing with a soccer ball. Not only did Nud dribble the ball exactly where it was supposed to go, but he would head it 'just like the professionals,' as one visitor exclaimed. As for jumping fences, we would just need to say 'rabbit' and he would be off! Typical of his breed, he had tremendous stamina and while I power-walked my daily 4 or 5km in this breathtaking area, Nud would cover another 20km chasing rabbits.

One of our guests from the UK often brought us a present and a new ball for Nud. He is without doubt the most photographed dog in New Zealand, perhaps in the southern hemisphere.

Rex used to kid us that Nud was not a real dog at all.

'He's a poncey dog,' he used to say.

Rex was an excellent shepherd himself and his dogs were well trained. One of them, a long haired Border Collie, was given a hard time by the older sheep dogs and suffered a dislocated shoulder. Rex planned to put

Our lovely Border Collie – Nud.

him down as he was now, 'no good for herding sheep'. So I suggested to Rex he let us have this dog instead of shooting him. Pronouncing his name, Spring, did not come easily for me as I could not roll my r's, so we re-named him Nick. Nud and Nick.

Everywhere Nud went, Nick went as well. I doubt Nick ever managed to touch the ball, but he had fun trying and gradually, together with a bit of TLC, he came right. So much so, that after a year I suggested to Rex he should take him back. After all, Border Collies don't come cheap and this one had the same intelligence and athletic traits as Nud. Rex, delighted to have his young dog back, changed his name back to Spring.

Prices for Merino at February's Lake Tekapo sale were reported in *The Timaru Herald* as being well up on the previous year.

The report went on to suggest that farmers might re-examine the amount of clothing they wear at work after a novel selling point was discovered at the sale. A pen of 12 ewes had been put up for auction by *Aoraki Naturally* – a clothes-optional homestay operation in the Mackenzie Basin. Bidding had stalled at $36.00 a head when a voice from the crowd asked; 'Do they come with a free weekend?'

Suddenly bidding moved briskly up to the eventual selling price of $41.

It was not clear whether the eventual buyer had any intention of attempting to claim a weekend at the homestay.

Brian was involved in Search & Rescue (SAR) as an advisor, and through his friendship with the local sergeant, Bill Apes, and various other contacts, he was on good terms with and well known to local police. On this particular day, one of his police friends decided to call and see us and so radioed in to base to advise his location.

'Oh, where are you going to pin your Police Badge?' queried the smart-alec from Timaru base.

'I'll just pin it to my Policeman's helmet,' came the quick reply.

Some weeks later we heard the distinctive *thump-thump-thump* of an Iroquois before we spotted it circling overhead and clearly defined a group of burly men, clad in bright orange overalls, sitting on one side, with feet hanging over the edge. The helicopter was thumping noisily by now and I yelled out to Brian, looking skyward, as were half dozen others nearby.

'Cripes, they're going to land!'

'Nah, they're just pretending to check us out. Let's do dead ants.'

So with that we all lay down on our backs and did dead ants lying on our backs waving our arms and legs in the air, while the Iroquois circled above, allowing the orange clad personnel on the other side a view of the antics below. It would have looked hilarious, given that we had nothing on except our shoes.

In an endeavour to get one over the police, who were on a cannabis recovery exercise, Brian phoned and left a message to 'complain' about the mis-use of an Air Force helicopter.

A couple of days later, Brian received a letter advising him of an SAR meeting, with a post script,

'You wear nice shoes, Brian'.

From time to time, a visitor, quite often from the Netherlands, would take one look at our *Shacklock* coal range and exclaim, 'Oh, I saw one of those in a museum'. So I would explain how economical they were, taking the chill off the kitchen on a cool day, heating our water and cooking meals, all at the same time. We would get buckets of apricots from Central Otago orchards quite cheaply. Each summer Brian would ferret around for his *Agee* preserving jars and bands and absorb himself in a similar ritual to our mothers.

Brian, bottling apricots from Central Otago

Feeling much like a homesteader one afternoon, there I was with a large saucepan on the coal range making apricot jam – my favourite. Out of the corner of my eye, I noticed a couple of flashes, so picked up the binoculars that were always sitting on the kitchen windowsill. The figure looking directly at me through binoculars in my sights, froze momentarily before ducking down behind a bush.

I popped outside and said to Brian and our neighbour, Robert, visiting from across the road.

'I think we have a Peeping Tom'.

Without any further ado, Robert jumped in his car with the cry, 'He's casing the joint; he's casing the joint'.

Meantime, a large black sedan careered out of Robert's drive and raced away out of sight. We thought it hilarious someone would spy on us in that manner.

There were occasions when it was necessary to be away for a few days. It was a quiet time, near the end of the season, with only a couple of visitors from Oamaru staying in their caravan up in the trees. Two young lads, aged about 15 or 16, drove in, did some wheelies in the near empty campground and drove out again. A few days later they were back for more wheelies. This time they stopped and got out of the car, dropped their trousers and urinated against a fence.

Unbeknown to these young lads, they were observed by our friends from Oamaru who, upon our return, sagely reported this misdemeanour together with the number plate of the car.

Brian phoned the local constable who said, 'Leave this with me, Brian.'

Nothing more was thought about it until he called in one afternoon to let us know the outcome. After locating the car's owner, he made an appointment with both children and their parents. He advised them they had in fact been observed driving into the grounds of *Aoraki Naturally*, near Lake Tekapo, on two occasions, and were seen behaving in an offensive manner by removing their trousers, showing their bare buttocks and urinating. This was a criminal offence.

The families were upset, knowing this could infringe on the further education or employment of their boys. The young constable said he had spoken to us and as long as there were no more problems during the next twelve months, they would not press charges. This was old style policing, as these lads who were from a neighbouring town, were just starting to become known to the local police and becoming a nuisance. Last report was, there were now two little angels residing in Pleasant Point.

Curiosity eventually got the better of a car load of dog-wallopers one afternoon (dog-walloper = young high-country musterer) on their way back from the dog trials. Our house was situated up on a ridge, so Brian had a clear view of their ute as it arrived at the fork in the driveway, opting to take the left hand track up to the sheds and the campground, instead of calling into the house first. Nud took this as his cue for more than the usual 'hello and welcome,' barks to his half dozen canine friends secured on the tray. Brian let the dog-wallopers go on up to the campsite and calmly drove down to the fork from the opposite direction, knowing full well what they were up to.

Meanwhile, a number of campers spotted our visitors, gave them a friendly wave and carried on yarning.

Now you have to wonder what would be going on in the heads of these lads at this time. Did they make out they wanted to camp for the night as they had been dared to do by other less courageous, but equally inebriated, dog-wallopers in the bar after the dog trials, or were they sheepishly (pun intended) going to drive out as if they had taken a wrong turning?

They chose the latter, and by that time Nud and I had walked down to the fork to hear Brian, trying not to laugh at these lads confronted with a totally naked woman, calmly asking the lads if he could help them. They were all extremely red-faced and apologetic, and even more red-faced when I suggested, 'Why don't you let me show you around the camp? That would be one up on the boys tonight in the bar!'

A nude highland fling in the high country. Mackenzie Muster 2002.

Walk on The Wild Side

A nude highland fling in the high country was no big deal for two cheeky Christchurch lads, who turned up unexpectedly at the beginning of January for the second annual *Mackenzie Muster Naturist Festival*, and while the two were new to the naturist movement, nudity apparently was already something of a habit.

Hamish Whelan told Sonja Rowell, Staff Reporter for *The Timaru Herald,* that curiosity brought him and his friend Ben Skelton, to the muster. The pair were already notorious among Christchurch acquaintants for their naked antics. Hamish was once thrown out of *Melbourne's Crown Casino* for wandering naked through the food court.

It was a quite different scenario wandering happily around *Aoraki Naturally*, wearing nothing but a hat and running shoes. Ben said, 'Nudity was a constant lifestyle choice.'

The pair were not shy about being photographed either, with *The Timaru Herald* showing the pair cavorting among the tussocks, each complete with a Scottish plaid over one shoulder. Shoes, hats and not a hell of a lot else were the uniforms du jour, as the *Mackenzie Bares Cross Country Fun Run* got underway.

Judging by the number of participants in the younger age bracket this year, it seemed that our event appealed to younger people like Hamish and Ben, who were keen to give organised nudity a go.

And while TAN editor, Les Rootsey, returned to successfully defend his title, the second place-getter, a younger Kiwi, was overheard telling the Aussie to polish the impressive trophy so he can see his face in it, when he takes it off him next year!

Photography is often a ticklish subject for many naturists, and even more so if the mere hint of a video is mentioned. Having my photo taken and published, whether it be clothed or unclothed, has never given me any cause for concern. After all it's nothing more than an image of what other people view. I have always been reasonably photogenic, and have lost count of the times my photo has appeared in naturist magazines.

Doug Ball used to say to me, 'You are my favourite nudist.'

To which I would reply, 'And you are my favourite photographer.'

New Zealand has some of the most spectacular scenery in the world, particularly the breathtaking backdrop at *Aoraki Naturally.* Why on earth wouldn't you want to take some holiday snaps?

I am conscious that not everyone feels the same way. There are many like Brian and myself, who enjoy promoting naturism and require good photographs to accompany information and promotional material. We are fortunate there are many naturists that are comfortable in their own skin and don't give a second thought to having their photograph taken.

Barely equipped . . . Russell Giles and Kay Hannam practise for the Great New Zealand Lawn Mowing Race. Photo, Sally Rae, *Otago Daily Times*.

Sally Rae could always be counted on for a great write-up and a creative, eye-catching photo. Her super sized colour photo captured the front page of the *Otago Daily Times* with the caption 'Barely equipped . . . Russell Giles and Kay Hannam practise for the Great New Zealand Lawn Mowing Race.'

A subsequent letter to the editor expressed the writer's distorted view that the photo was pornographic. Yet another expressed their concern about the harmful effects that nudity has upon children. I have yet to see any research substantiating that claim.

On the other side of the ledger, a respondent stated that people need to be reminded that there are still happy places left around the world. A further writer was even more inclined to think that society does more harm by its cover-up policy.

And while Anne Hatch's photo of a well-toned Ray Anderson from Invercargill warming up for the caber tossing event, may have had some tittering behind their hands, one wonders if it would have had the same effect on them had he been wearing a kilt.

Society has been conditioned to expect that genitals, and even women's nipples for goodness sake, should not be displayed in a daily newspaper. So it's not surprising that photographers have invented some very creative ways in which to portray people not wearing clothes, which has on occasions, had the negative effect of depicting subjects unfavourably.

In a clothes free environment, it's all a matter of commonsense and courtesy to ask people to refrain from taking photographs, unless of course you have the subject's consent. I have zero tolerance for surreptitious photography, particularly with the advent of mobile phones. Luckily, many of the people I meet share similar views. After all, it's a very good way in which to portray our lifestyle and we have always welcomed the media to our events.

So how did I handle a request from a Korean television crew wanting to film the action during the muster?

From our earlier email communication, I learnt they were preparing a documentary for *What a Wonderful World*, a cultural television programme. A documentary like never before, screened only in Korea.

I knew there would be a reasonable percentage of people more than happy to be in the video, but I was realistic enough to know there were just as many that would be horrified at the suggestion. I had reports of the same crew appearing unexpectedly on New Year's Eve at the national campout in *Rotota*, a naturist club near Rotorua, so a softly, softly approach seemed to be the most sensible solution.

When the crew eventually arrived in the evening, armed to the teeth with cameras and videos with zoom lenses, I suggested they leave their equipment in their van, and come with me into the marquee, where a pretty lively party was going on and meet everyone first.

By way of introduction, we also presented each crew member with a *Mackenzie Muster* tee-shirt and made it clear to everyone, including the crew, what our expectations were. I am a great believer in having my own agenda with the media, as they sure as hell have theirs!

Proudly wearing their *Mackenzie Muster* tee-shirts, the foursome were present for every kilted and un-kilted moment of the four day festival, and kept us entertained as well, filming events such as caber-tossing, lawnmower racing, warratah tossing and mallet throwing.

Several kilometres were clocked up between them as they were sighted dashing about between the tees in and around the golf course. The logistics of filming bare-backed horse trekkers around the picturesque base of Mount John became an even greater challenge for this intrepid film crew.

While the video was not screened in New Zealand (nor was it expected to be), reports that filtered out to me, showed it to be well received by Korean audiences.

Looking back through early newspaper cuttings, I came across my photo seated on the bank overlooking the creek, with the heading. 'A B and B laid bare.'

Newspapers work in different ways and an intriguing request came from the chief reporter of the *High Country Herald*.

'I need a reporter to do a feature, but it involves a walk on the wild side.'

This prompted an intrepid Sonya Rowell to head out for the high country to check out its latest attraction – to walk on the wild side – only to discover it was all quite tame, really.

A Love Affair with Swiss Rail and Other Fast Trains

With everything closed up for the winter, Brian and I planned to return to France again, extending our trip by a few extra weeks in order to explore other countries in the northern hemisphere.

Zurich beckoned for the first part of our journey. We were to be met by *Naspo Club* Vice-President, Ruth, who told us (once she figured out who the smiling couple were), that she was expecting two men. Kay is a man's name in many parts of Europe. This would have also been the reason our earlier email request to stay at another well known Swiss naturist club was ignored. Apart from banning the consumption of meat and alcohol, they did not allow homosexual couples!

With the earlier confusion out of the way, we were driven to park-like grounds surrounded by thick concrete walls. Thankfully, the variety of well established spruce trees camouflaged their modern security enclosure.

Our accommodation in a very large log cabin turned out to be rather like a sleeping room in a Marae, with eighteen beds all closely aligned to one another. We were the only visitors and expected something smaller. However we were pleasantly surprised when we saw every amenity was available in the well appointed kitchen, ensuring a comfortable stay.

The member owned club began in the 1930s and was set in a national park. Members could choose from outdoor table tennis (played on all-weather concrete tables), petanque and tennikoits. A large swimming pool and children's play area were located at one end of the grounds with spacious clubrooms housing a bar and social hall nearby.

Once in command of a good night's sleep and, having mastered the security locking system, a short walk outside the gate brought us to the local railway station. A quick check of the timetable and before long we were in Zurich central. This was really a practice run for the next day, as we planned to travel further to *Chateau Deau*, to stay with a Kiwi friend and his young family in their 17th century chalet.

This first train ride was the beginning of our love affair with *Swiss Rail*, and we made the most of our first class ten day *Eurail Pass*, through valleys and gorges, and high into the Alps.

One of our many excursions took us to Gruyere and, after the long climb to the huge Chateaux, we treated ourselves to double cream, served in a little chocolate cup, then poured into hot coffee. You then had the delicious choice of either stirring and melting the little cup in your coffee, or eating it whole. Of course we had another similar treat on the way back, and in my opinion the former is a far more decadent manner in which to enjoy your coffee.

Needless to say our next delicious foodie experience was savouring local cheese fondue. Brian contacted another friend, Monique, who had lived and worked in Lake Tekapo a few years before and she made us very welcome for an overnight stay. I was impressed with the way she made fresh muesli with her own fruit every evening, before retiring for the night. The addition of home made yoghurt served at breakfast time made it even more delicious – and good for you.

Gstaad is the land of the rich and richer, with price tags on some items of clothing amounting to that of my whole wardrobe, and my sisters' as well! I had to keep my sunglasses on, for by now my eyes were as big as saucers.

A quick sprint to catch the *Golden Pass* for Montreaux; then a leisurely trip on a 1910 paddle steamer, all on our first class *Eurail Pass*. Perhaps the most spectacular and unique journey was through to Grendelwold, with a bone shaking, clattering ride up the Jungfrau in a little cog-wheeled train, which took us almost to the top of Europe! Brian of course, is the mountain climber of the two of us, having climbed a dozen or more mountains of over 8,500 feet in New Zealand, but he had to agree the mountains of Switzerland were far more impressive, and certainly more accessible.

It was then time to meet up with our Italian friends Salvatore and Anna in Milano, and here is where the countryside changed from green valleys and wooden chalets adorned with geraniums, to a kaleidoscope of roofs and angles, buildings jostling for space in the city. Salvatore led us to the most popular pizza emporium, before joining yet another queue in order to taste some real Italian ice cream. Talk about titillating the taste buds!

We had been looking forward to renewing our acquaintance with Salvatore and Anna, whom we had met during our stay at *Le Vallon des Oiseaux* two years prior. Salvatore also wanted us to stay for a short time with his parents in their country home where we were treated royally, not just by his parents, but by the rest of the family, who also turned out in force to greet us. His Sicilian born mother did what came best, and cooked a mammoth meal for us and the twenty or so relatives seated around the crowded table, all speaking Italian, all at the same time.

But first we were to tackle Mont Blanc.

A series of cable cars, the outside temperature at each level several degrees colder than the previous one, brought us to our eventual destination, where we were almost blown away with the view and with the wind. We couldn't believe it when we came across an American couple in shorts and light sweaters, braving the chilly conditions.

We were definitely feeling like tourists now and another ride with our seemingly limitless *Eurail Pass* to Venice and a stroll around St Mark's Square, truly one of the most beautiful squares in the world, seemed an obvious choice to round off our sojourn in Italy.

Then it was back to Switzerland to Lausanne. Veronique and her partner Ard, who had visited us during our first season at *Aoraki Naturally*, re-located from Holland a number of years ago and were now living in a neat little village called Biere.

Coming from a country renowned for its increasing dairy herds, the gentle tinkling sound of forty or more cows making their way to the milking shed, brought us out onto the road. Brian managed to convey to the farmer the sharp contrast between hand milking his cows, and the mammoth structures back home in New Zealand.

Next day, waiting patiently for us at the TGV terminal outside of Avignon, was Arun, together with Elly, another good friend from Holland. Both spend their summer holidays at *Le Vallon*. Elly speaks several languages and helps out in the reception area. This doubles as a bar and takeaway outlet for the adjoining kitchen, as well as an area for taking orders and serving food and beverages on the terrasse, where grapevines enhance as well as provide shade for over sixty people seated in the outdoor restaurant.

For Brian and me, coming from New Zealand to the South of France to help Jan at *Le Vallon* for the second time, meant we continued to enjoy an endless summer. Our own naturist campsite was closed for the winter. Where better to spend the cold harsh months of the Mackenzie, than in sunny Provence. Trading minus ten for thirty-five degrees in the shade certainly doesn't take a great deal of encouragement.

We made the best of our free time and the companionship of a number of Dutch and British naturist friends on day trips to several historical places, including the *Pont du Gard*, a three level stone aqueduct crossing the Gardon river and which was built over 2000 years ago. We explored nearby Nimes with its impressive Roman amphitheatre, used as the setting for the film *Gladiator* and Fontaine-de-vaucluse, where 630 million cubic metres of water surge from its source every year. Although crowded, four of us strolled around the picturesque village before dining in the outdoor restaurant overlooking this beautiful stretch of water.

You can't help but wish to be a history buff, when you visit Castellane, the gateway to the Gorges du Verdon and travel on the historic Napoleon road, with its majestic plane trees.

Further excursions with Thjys led us to re-visit many of these unforgettable areas, including the city of Nice. Yes, it has a magnificent promenade, but it is not my favourite city. Marseilles on the other hand, held much more fascination for us both, as we explored the huge cathedral overlooking the Mediterranean port. On this occasion we were entertained by a young wedding party, with the photographer trying her level best to control their emotive display. What a fabulous backdrop for their wedding photos.

Hot temperatures were the norm during the summer months in Provence and we were looking forward to surprising our friends Roger and Vena during our day off. They had booked a chalet at *Belezy*, a short drive away, so with towels and nibbles packed, we set off looking forward to a day at Belezy relaxing in the sunshine. An ominous roll of thunder alerted us to the precipitation that followed. Manoeuvring our way through narrow cobbled streets alongside the deluge of water, windscreen wipers unable to keep pace, we eventually arrived at our destination. Slipping through the side gate at *Belezy*, we made our way across the sodden open space in front of the restaurant, heading in the direction of where we thought their chalet might be.

Drenched to the skin in light clothing and socks and sandals, we recognised them straight away; walking toward us for several paces before they realised who the two grinning antipodeans were. They had trekked over to the nearby village of Bedoin and back again and got caught in the unexpected downpour. Our afternoon culminated in a fabulous meal together in the restaurant.

Everything was slowing down at *Le Vallon*. The long weeks of school holidays in the Netherlands were finished; families were being replaced by a smaller number of retired naturists. Consequently, on some evenings there were fewer meals to prepare, with an early closing of the restaurant and bar.

There was a party and fireworks planned over two nights in the nearby village of Reillane. A number of staff members had gone to the party on the first night and our UK friends were keen for us to accompany them to the same party, still going strong, the following evening.

As there were only half a dozen meals booked and we could be finished early, I asked Jan before he headed off for his siesta, if we could finish at 9 o'clock that night. Unfortunately, I got the full effects of Jan's consumption of Genever during lunch, and he roared at me. Brian was stunned, as Jan, bearing down on me, ranted, 'I don't like the way you are speaking to me.'

'I'm not the one doing the shouting,' I said, trying to keep calm.

'You go!' he cried. 'You are finished.'

'We're not going anywhere.' I said. 'We have an agreement with you and we will stay for the duration of our contract.' Upon which he slammed out of the reception and locked us in.

After cleaning up the kitchen, and extricating ourselves through a small shuttered window, we explained the situation to our friends during our afternoon swim, before reporting to our usual posts at 4:00pm. In the kitchen, Brian was greeted by two young lads.

'What are you doing here?' He asked.

'We've come to cook the dinner,' came the reply.

'Oh, that's great.' Brian, handed the boys a bucket of onions, grinning; 'You can make a start on those.' Needless to say they were long gone by the time Jan put in an appearance.

We didn't go to the party and things simmered for a while. But it's amazing what a few smiles and a good night's sleep can do and before long, Jan was his usual affable self. In a week or so we would endure an emotional farewell.

NUDE WITH ATTITUDE

Dutch Treat

One of the regular guests at *Le Vallon* was due to leave for Holland around the same time as us, and offered a ride. Better still, he owned a BMW 5 Series Sport. Just a little guy; I didn't know whether to feel alarmed or amused as he braced himself up every now and then to look over the steering wheel. Brian, at 6ft and had no problem seeing the way ahead, shared the driving.

Even though we were on the high speed motorway, I was tempted to tap him on the shoulder when I saw the speedometer quivering at 170kph. We stayed overnight in a cosy gite, consumed some more delicious French cuisine then walked around the town square, soaking up the ambience of France for a few more hours, before setting off for Utrecht, where our friends Tineke and Nico lived.

Thousands of bikes parked in orderly fashion at *Utrecht Railway Station* indicated this was one huge city. 17 million people now live in the Netherlands, of which over 300,000 live in Utrecht. No wonder Dutch people had to be especially ingenious when building accommodation.

Tineke and Nico, who were regular visitors to *Le Vallon,* had invited us both to stay. They were planning a trip to New Zealand also, and were keen to find out the best places to visit and more about naturism in our country. Nico, like Brian, was a plumber and we all enjoyed a great friendship. Tineke was typically efficient and a capable hostess, as many Dutch women are. She operated a house cleaning business and it was great fun to visit with her, some of the beautifully renovated wharf side houses with their historic facades, many of which were located in buildings several hundred years old.

As is the case with many Dutch homes, their own home fronted on to the street with a rather large picture window where passersby, if they had a mind to, could see right inside through to the glass doors at the end of the room. Having lived several years in the country, I found it uncanny to be so close to strangers walking past while enjoying a meal at the dinner table.

Nico and Tineka had made the most of space in the spare bedroom by creating a mezzanine floor above the window, where a double mattress had been placed and we referred to it as 'sleeping in the campervan'.

Never one to sit still for long, Tineke spent a great deal of time with her extended family, including regular visits to an uncle ensconced in a rest home. Another night, we would be off to the local community hall for aerobics exercise.

Utrecht boasts an impressive organ museum which houses street organs, fairground organs, musical clocks and pianolas. Many of these were demonstrated as we walked through the museum. Brian and I did a little twirl on the polished floor, as this was no static museum. It was such a lively, happy place to be.

While in Utrecht, we cycled just about everywhere, along the picturesque canals, in awe of ancient architectural creations, then through flourishing landscape towards the *Pannekoeken Restaurant* which served beautiful, fluffy pancakes, with lashings of cream and caramelised apples. Just as well we were to bike home, as we devoured many calories that afternoon and even more during our stay, as Tineke cooked typical Dutch treats for us.

But isn't this the reason we travel?

In an endeavour to use up some more of those calories, we visited the Dom Tower which was built between 1321 and 1382, but balked at the thought of climbing the 465 stairs. In hindsight I wish we had as the view from the top of the tower would have been fantastic, though not if one of its thirteen bells rang. I was told they weigh between 800 and 18,000 lbs (360 and 8,160 kg).

May and Tom lived in Gorinchem and had visited us in New Zealand during the *Mackenzie Muster* in 2001. Tom drily reminded us of their frozen eggs and beer when the fridge thermostat in their rented van malfunctioned. The *Muster* was even more memorable for Tom as he celebrated his birthday during the weekend with an appreciable amount of *Wilson's Whiskey,* and in fact, won a large bottle to take home with him. Gavin, one of the Southerners, had taken them fishing on Lake Tekapo, as well.

We all enjoyed one another's company and, as was the case with our other Dutch friends, we were made very welcome in their home in Gorinchem, which was spacious by Dutch standards. This was a two storey block of four units with its own garage and only a short walk to Tom's allotment, complete with garden shed, picnic furniture and stream. Needless to say we met their extended family, a pretty lively bunch just like their parents.

Gorinchem dates back to the 13th century. The river Linge passes through the old centre, which is very well preserved and surrounded by 17th century earth ramparts. We very much appreciated Tom's knowledge of the historic defence systems, old mills, locks and canals. Tom, an authority on the water systems of the Netherlands, has since written a book about Holland's waterways, which was published shortly before his retirement. It's not surprising he was known as *Mr River*.

May, a company social worker, coped with what I imagine to be a hugely stressful job, where she listened to other's problems at a large manufacturing business, set up for disadvantaged persons. Work was provided for people of ethnic background, with little education and unable to get jobs anywhere else; many from Turkey and North Africa. She told me hers was the only office that allowed smoking. I imagine she would have heard and understood some horrific social problems during her working life. Yet, during a guided tour of the factory floor, we met many happy people.

On the Saturday night we were invited to a company barbecue party, which the whole staff from the CEO down and their families, attended. A small payment gave you a choice of delicious Dutch or Turkish food, with plenty of Amstel beer. For entertainment (when the dance band wasn't playing), we were treated to a polished performance by a professional Turkish belly dancer.

Travelling in the Netherlands was relatively simple, and our next stop was Amsterdam. Our hosts, Bab and Liesbeth, took us on a guided tour of their naturist club. This could only be reached by rowboat, moored alongside one of the numerous old mills that had been converted into a restaurant. We spent a very pleasant half day at the rustic naturist grounds and marvelled at the craftmanship of the old mill restoration.

Those of you who have visited Amsterdam before, will know of the ladies behind the windows. We had crossed the bridge and were being led by Bab to a bakery, 'to buy the best croquettes in Amsterdam,' when we heard someone call out, 'Brian, Brian!' Of course we all looked across the street, wondering who on earth knows Brian in Amsterdam, especially in this notorious street! Then we saw an excited Arun, running across the bridge. It turned out his plumbing business (yes, another plumber) was next door to the first of the ladies behind the windows.

We all agreed it was an unusual place to have a plumbing business and even more unusual for him to look up from his desk and see us crossing the bridge. He invited us up to his office for a cup of coffee, before we carried on to buy our croquettes and to continue our personally guided tour of Amsterdam, where over one million visitors go to the girls in the *Red Light District*.

We were still laughing about it when Bab and Liesbeith saw us safely on the train to *Schiphol Airport* for a short stop-over in Bangkok, where in Thailand, the restriction on daytime nudity is a paradox to the nightlife in Patpong.

A year before, we were entering a Bangkok restaurant for dinner when the terrible scene at the *World Trade Centre* towers in New York City, unfolded on the overhead TV screens. The terrorists altered the pleasure of overseas travel forever and it would never be the same again for any of us.

Orson Welles once said, 'There are only two emotions in a plane: boredom and terror.'

Give me boredom any time.

Touchdown at *Christchurch International Airport* in the fresh, clear air of New Zealand; Stanton waiting patiently with our car, then the long drive home to Lake Tekapo. Nud was in good condition and overjoyed to see us again. Before long he was back at soccer practice, while Ebony and Ivory assumed their rightful throne in the sun on the bank above Irishman Creek. In a short space of time we would roll the clocks forward for daylight saving, clean the birds nests out from *The Perches* and prepare for what was to be an eventful summer.

Four Workshops and a Wedding

Flying into Christchurch with the magnificent snow covered Southern Alps basking in sunshine, a glistening Aoraki/Mount Cook rose majestically above all other peaks: A welcoming beacon to our home below. After four months in the northern hemisphere, the Kiwis in France were back and in for a busy summer, culminating in our fifth birthday celebrations in April 2003.

A first for the Mackenzie, and indeed a first for a naturist resort, *Mackenzie Alpine Writers Retreat* in October, would be attended by writers from all over Canterbury. This was not a naturist event, however it presented an opportunity to connect and share ideas among our community. We hoped this would be a forerunner for other creative workshops at *Aoraki Naturally* and I had to admit to more than a cursory interest in writing. Having submitted various articles for several international naturist magazines promoting *New Zealand Naturism,* and increasingly, writing about our travels in Europe, one of my goals was to publish my memoirs. Like many others attending the writers retreat, I needed all the help I could get.

Having put the wheels in motion prior to our departure and with the assistance of local businesses who displayed promotional material, the workshops were given wide coverage and we were thrilled with the response. Earlier in the year, I had applied to *Creative Communities* through the *Mackenzie District Council* for funding, and we were able to provide two excellent tutors for what was to be a stimulating weekend, learning creative writing.

Maggi Danby-Belcher, from Christchurch, gave an informative presentation entitled *The Book*, featuring non-fiction and short stories. *Writing for Magazines* was the subject of a workshop by Karalyn Joyce, of Pleasant Point.

A number of our visitors stayed overnight and Brian took on the task of catering, with masses of piping hot savoury scones for morning tea and nourishing lunches for everyone. We fielded numerous questions during

Saturday evening's social Wine & Cheese, as our guests were understandably intrigued by our lifestyle and wanted to know more.

One woman who was planning a holiday in the South of France, seemed quite fascinated at the thought of swimming au naturel in the Mediterranean and was surprised to learn how many opportunities there were, even in New Zealand. A three course dinner was followed by a rousing evening of music and readings.

Following the second session of the workshops, and after everyone said their goodbyes, I was tickled pink to read a comment in our visitors' book: 'I'm only a towel away'.

Later that summer, we welcomed Paul and Diana from the United States. Paul had written to me asking for advice about their forthcoming holiday in New Zealand. In the process, he purchased a copy of *Holidays NZnaturally.* His next question took me by surprise somewhat, as he asked where would be the best place to get married – naturally!

I put my hand up, and quickly emailed our response, suggesting an early December wedding at *Aoraki Naturally*, when all the lupins were in flower, would be the most memorable day in their lives.

And it was. From the time they saw the bundle of pink and lavender balloons flying aloft from our letterbox, to long after they tied the knot. Ten years later, they are still buzzing about their day in the sun. Sometimes the simplest occasions can be the most significant milestones in one's life. And let's face it. *Aoraki Naturally* was kiwi simplicity itself.

Paul left all the arrangements for the wedding to me; flowers, wedding cake, music, food, marriage celebrant, even rent-a-crowd; a group of visitors staying on the grounds who eagerly joined in the festivities when I suggested a bottle of wine would go to the best dressed table in the colours of the lupins. Paul and Diana were also more than happy for me to put out a media release to the local press, who responded with reporter and photographer, Anne Hatch, from *The Timaru Herald*, arriving to record the afternoon celebration.

With wedding cake strategically placed in front of the newly married couple, the resulting colour photo depicted them wearing nothing but their birthday suits. As was marriage celebrant, Nelson Redshaw, who presented each with a *Pounamu*.

Anne reported in the *Herald* that Paul and Diana had met the previous November, while camping at *Laguna del Sol,* a privately owned naturist resort, in California.

'Meeting the way we did, takes away all the games – there is literally nothing to hide,' Paul said, and related how he found us through the internet. 'Everything just fell into place. Kay organised the whole thing and has been a real doll,' he said.

Residents of Placerville in California, Paul and Diana said that although they didn't want a big wedding, they didn't mind the publicity they had received. For Paul, naturism was a relatively new experience for him, and admitted that 'it was always me and clothes never really got along.' However the scout leader and soccer coach didn't dare 'come out of the closet'.

Paul and Diana Kircher cutting the cake after their wedding ceremony at *Aoraki Naturally*.

As a single father, he was mindful of anything out of the ordinary and was concerned that the state would jump at the chance to raise his child.

Diana was open and comfortable about her nudity, but was also mindful it was something that people didn't openly accept, and in most cases only tolerated. Consequently, only very close friends knew about their lifestyle. With this in mind, Brian took two sets of photos of the wedding; clothed and au naturel.

The article in the Monday paper piqued the interest of a local radio jockey, who telephoned for a bit of sport and cheekily asked me, 'What did they get up to, following the wedding?'

My response was to suggest he ask the groom himself, and handed the telephone to Paul.

'Oh, we just kicked back and relaxed,' was the tongue in cheek reply.

We still keep in touch, and three years following their visit to New Zealand, we enjoyed the pleasure of visiting them at their home in California.

No sooner had the dust settled and the happy couple were winging their way back to the US, than it was time to shake out the tartan and firm up our plans for the third annual *Mackenzie Muster*; now a regular event on the naturist calendar.

After weeks of searing heat and dark clouds all day Saturday, the Mackenzie skies opened up with much needed rain for the parched region. *Highland Games* were quickly changed to the *Lowland Games* in the Marquee, as Stanton laboriously dug a trench all the way round the perimeter in preparation for the *Tartan Tie 'n Boot Party*.

We had been very fortunate during the previous two years, as Brian McNab organised and spent the whole day ensuring the golf tournament was played according to the rules. This year, Lorna Inch, also a Lion's Club member and a good friend of ours, agreed to organise the tournament with the fees again going to the golf club. So it was a win-win for us and many sections of the community. Members of the *Lake Tekapo Lions Club* again prepared and smilingly served the buffet meal in the marquee, following the prize-giving.

Spot winners enjoyed scenic flights with *Air Safaris* and received several prizes from local sponsors. A number of visitors stayed on for Nude Horse-trekking with *Mackenzie Alpine Trekking Company* on the Monday. No bare back horse-riding for us though and we thoughtfully remembered our towels to cover the saddles. 'When your bum is bare, cover the rear.'

I eagerly read reports from several newspapers, thinking I should have a competition for the most ingenious caption. Regular visitor to the muster; reporter Sally Rae of the *Otago Daily Times*, led with the caption, 'A search for the bare necessities'; John Keast from *The Press* published a headline, 'Holidaying naturists give clothes the bum's rush'; while Ron Lindsay of *The Timaru Herald* came up with, 'Monty and Co enjoy naturist festival'. Yes, Monty was there again. In fact Monty is one of a select band of 'musterers' who proudly own all six *Mackenzie Muster* tee shirts.

Bare horse-back riding with Mackenzie Alpine Trekking Company. Photo David Jones.

Brian's photo appeared in The Timaru Herald the following Friday, installing his make-shift spouting with a bucket at each end, between the two marquees we had assembled. Oh, did I mention the rain?

January 2003 was especially memorable for me, as I became one of the few individuals awarded with the *Pat Trott Achievement* trophy for my dedication to the *New Zealand Naturist Federation.* I was pictured with the award in *The Timaru Herald*. The award, which was presented by the NZNF Treasurer during the *Mackenzie Muster* concert, came out of the blue, and was a very proud moment for me.

Riding on the success of the *Mackenzie Alpine Writers Retreat* and with the assistance of Lake Tekapo artist Shirley O'Connor, we came up with *Art in the Mackenzie*; two watercolour painting workshops to be tutored by Shirley, when the autumn colours of the Mackenzie would turn to golden hues and with snow on the Southern Alps, providing a stunning backdrop for the weekend.

Again *Creative Communities Scheme* supported our venture, which meant the registration fees payable were more manageable. By advertising two separate workshops; weekday and weekend, we received a surprising number of enquiries. This time quite a different group of participants arrived, many of them station owners throughout the district, which was exactly what the scheme was about; assisting people in the community to express their creativity.

Shirley came up with a program which saw the first part indoors in *The Compound*, where we learnt the basics of board, paper, and brush preparation, also instruction through the colour wheel. Several came close to replicating Shirley's *Church of the Good Shepherd at Lake Tekapo*, but we were being tutored by one of the best watercolour artists in the Mackenzie. We had a great deal to learn. But it was fun.

It was even more fun next day, when we went on location around the grounds. Sitting out at the back of the property, we learnt that with the subtle application of aquamarine – together with the correct outline of course – we could make a reasonable (and recognisable) replication of Aoraki/Mount Cook. Moving on to a stand of Silver Birch trees was even more challenging, but by the end of the session, with Shirley's enthusiasm and willingness to share her craft, the unanimous declaration was voiced, 'We can paint.'

When I look at Shirley's paintings gracing our own walls, I am reminded that each year Shirley would create a unique watercolour painting, depicting clothes-free participants enjoying events held during the *Mackenzie Muster*. Once completed, her partner Robin would frame it and donate it to the *Muster*. Raffle tickets for her colourful artwork were quickly snapped up during the weekend festival, with the proceeds donated to the *Mackenzie Highland Pipe Band.*

As with many of our activities at *Aoraki Naturally*, these workshops were reported in local media. We were delighted to learn also, that Shirley had won a second art award presented by the *South Canterbury Art Exhibition* for her painting entitled, *'Taking a Break'*, the first of a series depicting artists painting outdoors, battling the elements of nature at times. Shirley said she had received her inspiration to paint *'Taking a Break'*, from the watercolour workshops held at *Aoraki Naturally*, and the convivial atmosphere when artists relaxed at the end of the session with a glass of wine.

The past summer had been busy and interesting, full of great people. But it was time for us to again take a break and head for warmer climes.

With the silver birches finally shedding the last of their golden mantle, Nud was despatched to his holiday home in Irishman Creek Station. Ebony and Ivory would be snug in the now familiar cattery for the next four months and we would continue with our endless summer.

Introducing Two Kiwis who can Fly

It was a hectic weekend. The *Timaru Ladies Pipe Band* had planned a 50th reunion, and we were due to fly out the following day 2nd June. A reunion dinner held at *Seven Oaks Reception Centre* in Timaru, brought together dozens of my old friends. And as we poured over familiar photos, we found ourselves missing others unable or unwilling to be there. A celebratory street march with a jam session in the band room the following day, was where we truly excelled (or thought we did).

With a mixture of apprehension and excitement, we agreed to help at a different naturist resort in France for the height of the season. Suzanne Piper had suggested we contact Xavier Feraut, at *Domain de L'Eglantiere* in the Pyrenees. Sue agreed it would be a completely new experience for us, working with a French family. She knew the family very well and felt we were up to the challenge. Xavier and his family spoke English and so our email communication firmed up the time of our arrival in early July.

In the meantime, having done our research, we were on our way out of *Charles de Gaulle Airport* in our newly acquired Peugeot 206, when we came across a young family from New Zealand, stressed to the max, unsure which route to take.

'Follow me,' said Brian. What a hoot, Brian showing others how to get out of Paris. But he did, then fuelled up and headed south, easily finding our overnight stop at *Moulin de la Ronde*, a picturesque naturist campsite, near Vierzon in the Loire Valley.

Our route took us through Clermont-Ferrand to Rodez and a beautiful Dutch owned campsite. *Le Fiscalou* is set in 14 hectares of rolling woodland, with a variety of campsites in sun and shade. Settled in an onsite caravan, we headed for the swimming pool and bar where we ordered a generous sized pizza for dinner.

With another week to explore, we found interesting towns such as Cahors, in the centre of the Lot valley and where we boarded a little train next to Pont Valentre; a lovely way to see Cahor and an easy manner in which to view the mediaeval cathedral and other interesting places in the town. The train is unique as it runs on wheels on the road.

Worth viewing, if only from a distance, was the classic hill town of Brunequil. Parking at the bottom of a hill we walked to the top of the fortified Cordes Sur Ciel. Strolling through the picturesque town of Millau, Aveyron's second largest city and the home of *Roquefort* cheese, we also learned Millau is famous for the manufacture of quality handmade gloves. On our return visit some years later, we would cross the beautiful Millau viaduct on its completion.

French naturist resorts are sometimes difficult to find, but by close inspection of our *Michelin* map, we eventually located our destination near Castelnau, in the midi Pyrenees. Nervous about meeting the family for the very first time, we drove into *L'Eglantiere* and pulled up outside the closed reception. A dark haired woman and a young teenage girl standing beside her, waved out to us from outside a very large building, which turned out to be an expansive restaurant and bar on the terrace, above a beautifully landscaped and sheltered swimming pool which I couldn't wait to immerse myself in. I was to spend nearly all my leisure time when we were not exploring the region, either swimming in or lazing around this beautiful facility.

Eventually Marcella, the Dutch partner of Xavier, and her daughter, Iris, drove around in a golf cart and greeted us effusively with kisses on our cheeks. I guess the *All Black* flag in the window of the Peugeot must have been a dead giveaway as no introduction seemed necessary, with Marcella explaining the family were a little nervous about meeting two Kiwis.

Marcella, in gregarious mood, tore around the large campsite in her pink golf cart with the two of us hanging on for dear life, and found what was thought to be the perfect site: slightly elevated and well protected from the wind, with quite dense shrubbery around all sides of the spacious sites; within cooee of the restaurant and best of all, only a short stroll to the Sanitaire. Later, during the evening, we were to meet Xavier and the rest of the family.

In no time at all we had pitched our two person igloo tent, which was to be home at *L'Eglantiere* for the next six weeks.

Arriving prior to the busiest time of the season meant a flurry of activity in *Le Epicerie*, where I was to spend most of my day. The little supermarket, situated beneath the large restaurant and bar area, stocked all manner of food and beverages, fruit and vegetables. Cleaning and stocking shelves were prioritized, with several large pallets of merchandise to be put in place before opening day.

Xavier's mother, Marcelle, a retired school principal, often joked she had eyes in the back of her head, and became a good friend. After swimming my early morning K in the pool, I would greet her in the traditional French manner with kisses on each cheek, 'Bonjour Marcelle!' as she counted all the newspapers.

I would stock the fruit and vegetables. My next mission was to tally the mountain of French bread and croissants. First rule, keep the suppliers honest.

L'Eglantiere is chosen by many of the thousands of Dutch families who visit a wide variety of French naturist centres, during their summer vacation. Then it is the turn of the French to go on holiday. That's when my communication skills were put to the test. Luckily Marcelle is a whiz at languages – nine in all. She took great delight in translating my Kiwi accented English to assist rather puzzled customers. After all, it was a bit of a surprise to find someone from New Zealand behind the counter!

We were to learn more of this difficult language through *Conversations with Maurice*, held twice a week and giving me the confidence to count, as well as greet people in French.

Le Epicerie closed at midday and I usually tracked down Brian before lunch, which was invariably followed by siesta. He had delegated himself the job of keeping all the sanitaires clean and in good order, after spotting Xavier at midnight one evening hard at work hosing out the showers, explaining he had no-one else to do the job, the previous cleaner having made up her mind not to continue. Brian's mind on the other hand, must have worked pretty quickly on this one, as it meant a lie-in each morning. Juggling cleaning between the odd spot of maintenance, plumbing, cooking lunch for the personnel on the chef's day off and catering for the barbecue on Mondays, he was one happy chappy.

In fact, Monday lunch was sure to attract all the personnel eager to sample Brian's culinary skills, and his attention to presentation was always appreciated. Monday evening was another opportunity for Brian's promotion up the food chain to be put to good use, preparing the weekly barbecue for up to 100 guests.

Prior to the barbecue, Xavier presented an overview of the surrounding area and, with a welcome drink for all the new visitors having arrived on Sunday, introduced the personnel, including the two kiwis who can fly and don't like winter. Coming from New Zealand, having our own naturist campsite and enjoying an endless summer, was an opportunity Xavier took great delight in telling others about. Needless to say, we basked in the limelight, with numerous additions to our extended naturist family becoming firm friends.

Top to bottom: Over-looking the swimming pool at L'Eglantiere; Xavier welcomes visitors to L'Eglantiere; Kay with Marcelle in the Epicerie; Brian and Kay serve salads at the Monday night barbecue.

Days off each Sunday saw us tootling around neighbouring regions in our little Peugeot, stopping at sleepy little villages for lunch, or picnicking on the side of the road. Six weeks went very quickly. It was a mad rush to pack up everything and stash it away for the following year. Yes, they wanted us back and what's more, there was the promise of a caravan to stay in.

An hour's drive brought us to *Pau Airport*, where we dropped off the car and flew to London. Catching the train from *Heathrow* was fine, but the descent on the flight of steps was traumatic, as I was jostled and lost my balance. I just about fell down the steps, then realised my laptop had been knifed from its secure position atop my bag. What a bloody nightmare! Brian was about ten steps ahead of me. Where was that man when I needed him? I was almost paralytic, sobbing my heart out as I screamed out to him.

There was nothing we could do other than report it to the police. I was very concerned about the personal information contained on my laptop. However, I was reassured by the young constable, it was generally known that thieves would strip all the files to ensure the laptop was clean when they went to sell it.

I was still blubbing by the time we met Roger and Vena, whose calm and compassionate manner soothed my troubled behaviour. On several occasions during the years which followed, we would enjoy their boundless hospitality and companionship, each time urging them to re-visit New Zealand where we could return their kindness.

We had arranged to meet Jack and Jane Head, who had kindly promised us the use of their campervan for a two week tour. From Wainfleet, Jack and Jane were regular visitors to New Zealand and stayed with us at *Aoraki Naturally*.

Merryhill Leisure, set in 22 acres and surrounded by woodland in a lovely corner of Norfolk, was our next stop. After settling in, we made our way down to the pool to say hello to others enjoying a swim.

With quick introductions all round, a woman then said to me, 'So you're Kay Hannam, we've heard about you. We're coming to New Zealand next year and want to buy your guide.'

The easiest way to see nearby Norwich was to drive to the large car-park, take the bus to the centre and board a local bus – as we often did in other big cities – sitting up front with the driver to get the lowdown on the city. Did you know Norwich is famous for the manufacture of mustard, and Waterloo Park has one of the longest herbaceous borders?

With a father by the name of Lloyd George Williams, Brian felt it only right that we should visit Wales. We were not disappointed and could have spent another two months exploring this glorious country, through lush green valleys with magnificent landmarks and old stone cottages.

Thything Barn is located on the Carew River on the site of a now defunct oyster farm, and afforded plenty of opportunities to explore the foreshore and tidal areas, with wonderful walks in what can only be described as a naturist woodland. We gladly accepted the invitation to stay an extra night. It was plain to see why Pembrokeshire is a favourite location for artists and photographers.

Up through the valleys and to the top of Mt Snowdown at 1,085 metres, the highest mountain in Wales, via a track and pinion railway, before visiting a fascinating exhibit detailing the history and development of hydro-electricity; underground Eliden Mountain and Europe's largest man-made cavern, where some of the world's most powerful hydro-generators operate. Having worked at an underground power station at Manapouri years ago, Brian was especially intrigued with the generators which can go from zero output to full power within seconds. There is no water waste, even though an incredible amount of water passes through the pump storage system from the lake above, and back again.

Driving through the landscape, we could not help but be moved by rows and rows of miners' cottages, before crossing a little privately owned bridge which requires a ten pence toll. While the families are still alive, it remains a toll bridge.

Portmeirion village, a fanciful but real-life filming location for *The Prisoner* viewed on our television sets in the 1960s, led us to believe we were somewhere on the Mediterranean.

No visit to Wales would be complete without a visit to the impressive Caenarfon Castle where we were caught up in the latter stages of a festival, and where I learned of all things, how to make a felt hat!

Completing our Welsh Oddysey in Wye Rexom, we booked ourselves into a bed & breakfast before a most memorable meal at *Wye Kaban*. A drunken brawl outside one of the local pubs quickly changed our plans of having an after dinner drink there; opting instead for a rather plain looking establishment, but crowded inside. In spite of our long and earnest protestations, we were roped in to a team. It was Pub Quiz night. Answering the questions correctly was bad enough, deciphering the language was quite another!

Mason Jars and the Devon Mafia

I must have had a sudden rush of blood to the head during the summer, as I found myself appointed Communications Officer and back on the NZNF Executive. The federation had completed its rebranding with the new *gonatural* logo, created by a Wellington design company, with the slogan grin and bare it, since changed to for health and well-being, with a new website www.gonatural.co.nz. The logo depicted an adult couple together with a child, above the word *gonatural*. Anchored below was a blue and white towel, often the only thing carried by naturists.

The branding was professional and well developed, providing an even better platform for naturist clubs in particular, to gain a credible market presence. There was also an opportunity to market *gonatural* products on behalf of the NZNF, which initially, I agreed to sell. However, while I fully supported the *gonatural* brand, in my view *Aoraki Naturally* was already following the philosophy and implementing the core values behind the brand, which I felt some clubs were not adhering to. It was more than having a fancy logo, which really did not sit well with our own business as we had already established ourselves with a good recognisable brand name, together with a very popular website.

Even the manner in which visitors just rock on up to our front door is far removed from the process prospective visitors to some clubs had to endure for many years before switched-on members began introducing new initiatives. Their experience usually occurs when they come across the concept and think it might be a good fit. Naturally they want to find out more information. How that process is carried out, determines what their next step is. It shouldn't be made out to be a big deal; after all, they just want to try something that is bound to be good for them. We know that already, so why put any obstacles in their way?

Our welcoming approach to visitors brought an even younger demographic and a bigger crowd than the previous year, to our annual event in January; the parched brown landscape of the Mackenzie Country providing the perfect backdrop for young families wearing nothing but smiles, during the four day festival.

Our recipe for success stayed pretty much as in other musters. Dubbed the wildest ever, some might view naked pole dancers as being little risqué, but they were not there to see the fun, were they?

But the best was yet to come. We settled down for the evening's entertainment.

Ever performed team lip sync?

Songs chosen from a CD given to each 'clan' on arrival, contributed to the hilarious finale. The rules were, you had to choose one song and could only use props found in and around the grounds.

Most original went to *The Oldies* led by Les and Laurel Olsen, for their enactment of the Beatles number, *Help is on its way*. Picture this: Two old ladies circle a pond (paddling pool) on the ground of the marquee. One old lady falls down and seemingly breaks a leg. Les, with arms waving like a propeller and wearing WWII flying goggles, and Laurel, complete with what appears to be a white nurse's apron and cap, stitched with a bright red cross, 'fly' around, circling the pool. The next action appears unbelievable, as two stretcher bearers trot around the pool, then lift the old lady with great decorum onto an old khaki army stretcher.

It's simply amazing what you can find in Brian's shed!

No sooner had the plane landed and the applause died down, when we heard a shriek from outside the marquee, as the next group practiced their routine. It was Amy, in hysterics about performing nude on stage. A rendition of the *Nude Macarena* by the clan of six brought the house down (or marquee in this case), and an even more hysterical Amy off the stage almost, to a raucous call of 'encore'!

While holding the *Mackenzie Muster* each year may seem as something of a habit, we were also making preparations for our annual trip to Europe, to spend two months of the northern summer again at *L'Eglantiere* in France.

Our first port of call however, was to Los Angeles to meet Paul and Diana, who lived in Placerville, previously known as Hangman's Town, where thieves and murderers swung by the neck during the gold rush days. Masses of yellow ribbons and Stars & Stripes were tied to trees, telephone poles, gates and doorways along the way. However, they had substituted their banner for the New Zealand flag which graced the front entrance of their country home.

Brian is never one to sit still for long and immediately put Paul's brand new chainsaw to good use, soon having a supply of firewood stacked away.

Paul and Diana were effusive hosts and we were constantly 'on the go', visiting other quaint towns in the region. Wandering around the tiny foothills town of Georgetown, Brian popped into a tavern and ordered a beer. He was a bit taken aback when his drink arrived in a screw top jar and queried the barman.

'This here's a Mason jar, sir,' The barman drawled. 'It's how we serve our beer.'

Paul had arranged for us all to visit *Laguna del Sol*, a large clothing-optional resort where the four of us rented a roomy cabin. Earlier in the day, we visited *Wal Mart* to find something for the *Patriots Party* that evening. I found some red, white and blue sparkly headgear for Brian and me, and was surprised to see Diana buy bra & knickers in army camouflage. Apparently that's how they do things in some nudist clubs in the States. Determined not to feel uncomfortable, we just enjoyed the music and the dancing, ignoring the fact many were in – or almost out of – their underwear!

Eventually we arrived in London, another grateful stopover, courtesy Roger and Vena, beginning with a post-dinner swim and spa evening at *Coghurst Hall* to fend off the jet-lag. Given the opportunity to see the major tourist sights around London, we made an early start, rewarded with the lunchtime *Changing of the Guard*, at *Buckingham Palace* and a superb view of the city from the *London Eye*.

Set in the grounds of a country manor house in Buckinghamshire, is *Diogenes Naturist Club*, where we were invited to pitch our tent in their pretty English garden. We both felt *Diogenes* had tremendous potential for hosted accommodation, but the members preferred the traditional camping style. Formed in the 1930s and in its present location since 1964, *Diogenes*

Top: Vena and Kay at Coghurst Hall; Bottom: Vena and Roger outside their home in Eltham, London.

has numerous petanque pistes, miniten courts, children's play areas and boasts an outdoor pool as well as a large heated indoor swimming pool, adjacent to the superb manor house.

Two of the oldest established naturist clubs were also on Roger's list. *The Naturist Foundation* in Brockenhurst, offers the largest and best equipped club within the Greater London Boundaries, and is just a few minutes from the M25.

Diogenes Naturist Club, Buckinghamshire.

Speilplatz, founded in 1929 in Bricket Wood, a little corner of St Albans, is the oldest UK naturist resort. *Speilplatz*: An unlikely name for an English naturist club, its Germanic beginnings being the likely reason. A year round residential club, where our host, Suzanne Piper lived, its facilities included a heated swimming pool, Solarium, sauna and licensed bar. We had been invited for lunch. However, the cook had thrown the pots and pans in the air. So guess who cooked lunch? Brian might be the local plumber, but he's a handy feller to have around when folk are hungry.

But, we had a train to catch, to acquaint ourselves with the setting of many of Agatha Christie's novels and to meet the Devon 'mafia', waiting to show off the best of Devon's heartland.

My last visit to *Stonehenge* in 1986 afforded a close-up view, but this time we were faced with large, high-security fencing, and an even higher fee to gain entry.

The first address included the intriguing description of *Middlebarn*. The middle of a stone barn had been converted into three quaint dwellings and while space was at a premium, our hosts devised creative ways in which to store their belongings. Understandably, we slept on the floor next to the piano. Crowded on the little terrace for an evening barbecue with members of the 'mafia', we were given clues about our next destination. Talk about mystery!

Woodbury provided accommodation in a delightful little wooden cottage at the bottom of a *Burgage*, a medieval land term, which usually consisted of a long and narrow plot of land with the narrow end facing the street. The wider end opened out onto a common meadow in which the neighbourhood's cattle grazed. Within walking distance, restaurants afforded us a wide range of locally produced food. Arriving back well before dark, a fairly convivial hour or two playing lawn badminton and socialising on the adjacent deck of a small outside sauna, followed. The more red wine our hostess consumed, the broader became her expressions of, 'Oorright! Oorright!' Until I could barely understand what she was saying.

Next to play 'mine host' to their kiwi friends were Blair and Janet of Kingsbridge, where we made the most of walking opportunities and explored several beautiful coastal towns. At Slapton Sands a large, black, painted tank drew our eye, and we were informed of an incident in 1943, when Slapton Sands – similar to a beach in Dunkirk – was used as a training ground. Coordination and communication problems resulted in 943 American allies killed by friendly fire and German E-boats.

Our arrival back in London afforded a short breather before heading across the channel ourselves, only this time by air with a brand new Peugeot ready to go in Amsterdam, booked months ahead and very convenient for our travels in Europe. We immersed ourselves in Dutch culture by celebrating the Orange progress through *World Cup Football* at a neighbourhood party with May and Tom, before heading south to France.

The entrance at Domaine de la Gagère.

Domaine de la Gagère is situated in the Burgundy region in the centre of France, easily accessible from many parts of Europe. From small beginnings in 1993, *La Gagère* offers 4-star 'Camping de Qualité', offering 120 large campsites, most of which have electricity, plus a wide variety of rental accommodation.

Football fever was rife here also, with a colourful string of Orange pennants around the restaurant area. Quite unexpectedly, the barbecue that evening hosted by owners Tom and Betty, was accompanied by some lively Belgian musicians.

As was often the case when it became known that Brian was a plumber, a job offer invariably came his way. Next thing you knew he was repairing the pump.

Breaking new ground further south in the Dordogne, we visited *Le Couderc,* a charming naturist campsite run by Olivier, Nico and Marieke, who live on the campsite with their families.

Memories of a large Mas which housed reception, bar and restaurant, also remind me of the dappled sunlight from grapes happily growing above while I participated in one of their regular art workshops.

Though our stay was all too short, *Le Couderc* is one of those places marked, 'must return soon'.

Art workshop at Le Couderc

Before long we were ensconced in a caravan adjacent to the restaurant and kitchen at *L'Eglantiere*. Although a new team of personnel were on hand, we saw many familiar faces of both Dutch and English people during the next two months. I was soon transformed into *Madame Epicerie*, while Brian turned his hand to all manner of maintenance and for the pleasure of us all – preparing the personnel lunches and the Monday evening barbecue.

In addition to numerous friendships established, I was charmed by a number of special little friends, including Hannah from Belgium, who painted several masterpieces for me to adorn the epicerie and Merel from the Netherlands, smiling at me with her two front teeth missing, requesting, 'un baguette, cinq croissants and un *Volkstrant* (a Dutch newspaper),' each morning.

Young members of the *Miniclub* next door were earnestly putting finishing touches to their craft, while the older children were catered for with activities such as totem pole building, table tennis, volleyball or raft racing, with ghost hunting evenings and weekly concerts the more popular events of the summer.

Not a week would go by during the height of the summer season, without some form of musical entertainment for all, the most memorable being the *Paella* night, complete with *Flamenco* dancers.

We were feeling quite at home with 'family Feraut'.

Croatia in the Buff!

One of the questions I am often asked is, 'Do you have meetings in the nude?' My response is invariably determined by the temperature at the time. While attending a meeting in a naturist environment, whether it be a discussion group or national council meeting, to enjoy the freedom from clothes somehow feels right to me. One would expect also that at an international meeting, a relaxed state of dress (or undress) would apply. Weather permitting of course.

At two previous INF World congresses in Sweden and Germany, cold weather dispelled any expectations I may have had beforehand of a large formal meeting of international representatives in the buff. So you can imagine it was with absolute disbelief after arriving in Croatia for the INF World Congress, with temperatures around the balmy 30s, to be told not only did the management of Valalta Naturist Resort insist on all delegates and guests being dressed for meals, but during the meetings as well!

President Wolfgang Weinrich wrote in his press release prior to the 29th INF Congress;

'Organised naturism is facing new dimensions,

The social attitudes in many nations have changed, naked swimming in many places has become normal, associations and clubs have seen a reduction in membership. New structures are required, because the situation where naturism required protected places is no longer necessary.

How should the worldwide union of the naturist federations react? Can powerful structures be created? Is a crisis management necessary? And an important question: what will be the role of commercial naturism in the future?'

The host for the 29th INF Congress is the *Valalta* resort, a naturist holiday centre, according to the press release, 'Where the management encourage and remind clothed people to respect naturism, and in which nudity is paramount.'

Some one had shifted the goal posts. As far as I could see, there was not a naked body in the room.

A difficult beginning, which soured the initial enthusiasm of many delegates. The election of officers and the laborious task of going through all the articles in the statutes, also took far longer than necessary. There was much discussion of the terminology nudism/naturism or was it naturism/nudism. My own reminder to the Congress that we in New Zealand had spent considerable time and effort educating the general public to accept the words naturist and naturism, was met with a round of applause from some delegates, including those representing France and Belgium.

When the meeting finally disbursed for a break, there was a beeline for the complex of large salt-water pools, or directly to the beach. And what a beach! Not your usual sandy, dusty beach, but calm, clear and warm, with a wide expanse of creamy coloured rock sloping into the water, ideal for sun-lovers. I was able to swim the two hundred or so metres to a buoy line. This prevented the passing parade of ferries, yachts, power boats and jet-skis from entering the area, ensuring the safety of thousands of naturists swimming in the salt-laden sea.

Accommodation at *Valalta* was in one of several one or two bed-roomed apartments, with few facilities other than a separate bathroom and a nice deck leading onto a courtyard. Ours was serviced daily, with linen changed and all tile floors washed, inside and outside. The Congress included all meals for delegates in a large dining room which reminded one of its totalitarian beginnings.

As at any international gathering it's wonderful to renew acquaintances with old friends from far away countries, establish future communication lines and new friendships such as the Croatian and neighbouring Slovenian delegations. We were invited to join this group of friends for their end of year meeting at nearby *Monsena*, following the Congress.

Monsena is one of several large naturist centres promoted by the Croatian Tourism Board. Sadly, we learnt this lovely beachside resort had new owners and would be 'textile' as from October.

On the second storey of our concrete apartment, we were spoilt with an incredible vista along the Istria Peninsula; across to the picturesque town of nearby Rovinj and of course the constant passing parade of watercraft.

A fridge meant the wine could be cooled when required and the cheese prevented from spoiling. Breakfast and dinner were included in a very reasonable overnight tariff, and feeling thoroughly rested, we looked forward to the weekend with our new friends.

This time, however, the meeting was more to our liking. Lazing around with just a hat on, while everyone played volleyball or enjoyed a game of Petanque under the shade of the birches. Rather like home really!

Speaking of the birches, that's where we were heading next. Situated just 25km from the centre of Turino in Italy, *Club Le Betulle* (The Birches), boasts an enviable geographical locality, surrounded by green hills and within walking distance of the small town of La Cassa.

The club was founded by its present owners in 1969 and is one of seven naturist clubs in Italy, affiliated to the INF.

Gianfranco and Luisa were not strangers to us, having met them at previous INF Congresses. So it was with typical Italian hospitality we were welcomed late at night, after leaving Croatia in the morning. As is the case in many European motorways, never ending congestion resulted in an after dark arrival to the district. However, by enlisting the help of the local Carabinieri, we were afforded a guided escort to the electronically operated entrance of *Le Betulle*.

Top: Volleyball at Monsena, Croatia; Bottom: Le Betulle members pride and joy - their gardens.

Following the lights and the distinctive hum of foreign voices, we made our way to *The Chalet*, an indoor/outdoor family restaurant where a large number of Dutch campers were enjoying a meal together.

After the first question of, 'where can we please stay?' was resolved, there came the next, 'have you eaten?' It soon became clear the generous meal we avidly consumed was pretty much par for the course, with members contracted to operate the restaurant on a regular basis. We were to learn also that not only were lunches and evening meals available, but breakfast as well. Brian enviously acquainted himself with the commercial style kitchen, fitted out with sparkling stainless steel equipment. A far cry from any club house kitchen we've ever come across!

Our first night's accommodation was spent in a comfortable older style cabin, complete with small bathroom and kitchenette. An initial daylight exploration revealed several more well constructed chalets of varying sizes, also caravans available for hire. The vans themselves were used for sleeping quarters; a wooden extension constructed in treated pine, completely sealed, with wooden floor and double glazed windows, provided the kitchen/dining area. Beautifully nestled on the hillside, among the birches and oaks, the caravans, to all appearances, resembled log cabins in among the birch trees. Over-looking the splendid swimming pool, club house, office and solarium, we determined a caravan ideal for a few more days than we had originally intended.

You may have gathered by now that *Le Betulle* is sited on several terraces, the lower area complete with car park and camping areas. It came as no surprise to us that our car was to be left in a separate area. While this might prove tedious for some, it certainly ensures quiet camping. No noisy engines or car doors slamming all times of the day and night.

In spite of cooler weather than we had experienced in Croatia, I immersed myself in the pool and powered several lengths to unwind from the previous day's journey. Now, with the sun warming our bodies, our skin absorbing a natural dose of vitamin D, we relaxed on a large terrace built on top of the Club House. With perimeter walls for protection from the wind, we chose from the range of sun-loungers, tables, chairs and beach umbrellas provided.

Members and guests alike stored their belongings in a personal locker in a spacious dressing room, kept up their fitness on gym equipment and relaxed in the sauna. A shower and toilet was provided in this area also. Adjacent, a large meeting room housed a library, billiards, coffee and bar facilities.

Outside, and to complete the sporting facilities available in this year round club, were table tennis, volleyball, and mini tennis courts. The archery course located at the top level is where we viewed the panorama of woods and valleys below.

We spent a memorable day in Turino, having first parked our car in a village nearby and caught the local bus into the city. Our sightseeing included the *Musee of Cinema*, which depicted a variety of static and moving displays of films and filmstars, classics from a bygone era. From the highest vantage point in the city, also located in the musee, we were able to look out over the myriad of rooftops and landmarks in the city.

Taking advantage of the commercial aspects of their locality, the club leased several of their accommodation units to visitors during the 2007 Winter Olympics. We enjoyed several excursions in the surrounding countryside, such as the Valle di Lacana during our short stay and both agreed this is a magical place, in winter and summer.

It was to be a further three weeks before we eventually arrived home. I was looking forward to another meeting; our own NZNF Council meeting, where I would give a full report of the INF Congress. In the buff!

No Clothes Attached

Although I endeavoured to ensure our commercial enterprise worked in a symbiotic relationship with other member organisations, I eventually withdrew from the brand promotion and concentrated instead on setting an example which others could follow, rather than trying to direct club committees.

Significantly, during the past fifteen years since Joan and Kevin Sampson, Brian and I, and some owners of naturist home stays, have opened our doors to the general public, there has been a definite change of attitude, with New Zealand member clubs being far more pro-active in implementing positive ways in which to attract visitors.

It was certainly easier to work in our own corner, learning from other operators in the tourism sector, yet still retaining the core naturist values and putting ourselves out into the public arena.

Mackenzie Muster was by then the biggest promotional event for naturism in New Zealand, not a large gathering by world standards and admittedly not the biggest gathering of naturists. Our November press release, targeting media nationwide, nevertheless netted an enthusiastic response. Several dailies featured news of the fifth annual Scottish frolic held at our scenic grounds.

Our biggest pre-muster surprise was the arrival of a young reporter, Nell Husband, in her trademark *The Timaru Herald*, black Nissan.

'Can I please come to the muster?' Hesitating, unsure of our reaction to her request.

'Of course,' we enthused. 'We usually welcome a number of journalists while the muster is on.'

Nell continued, 'But can I take part, and can I bring Grace, my daughter? She's only five. Lindsay, my partner might come too! He's not a naturist though, is that okay?'

No prizes for guessing our response!

During the course of our interview over a companionable cuppa, Nell disclosed her affinity towards our own chosen lifestyle. 'Oh, Grace and I do this sort of thing at home pretty much all the time. Some of my colleagues will probably give me a hard time, but I'll cope with that.'

We were to learn that Lindsay, also an astute journalist and editor of *Community High Country Herald*, had body acceptance issues to deal with. During their last visit to *Aoraki Naturally* some weeks (and visits) later, Brian quipped, 'I'm a bit worried about you Lindsay, that's the second time you've forgotten your bathing costume.'

'Ah well,' responded Lindsay, applying copious amounts of sunscreen. 'That's what happens when Nell packs your suitcase'.

I digress. However, it's not everyday we have a real live journo actually participating in our naturist festival and promising to write a feature article in our local daily newspaper!

The familiar blue and white marquee was up and the decibel level of the 'gathering of the clans' a comfortable hum. Large tables groaned under the weight of a delectable variety of food. Tucking in, we rubbed shoulders, some bare, with friends from Australia, the Netherlands, Great Britain, as well as North Islanders who had travelled south from the *NZNF Rally* at *Pineglades* a week earlier, to join us mainlanders.

Entertainment manager Tony Wheeler, veteran of earlier musters, was ready at the microphone as two hundred rosy cheeks (the facial variety) turned expectantly for the first of the 'quizzes'. They were all in good form. Brian and I shared a quiet sigh of relief in spite of the ominous clouds and spectacular thunderstorm southeast.

A flash of tartan and glimpse of pristine white painted spats outside indicated the arrival of the *Mackenzie Highland Pipe Band*, assembled ready to pipe in the haggis. Unbelievable! Not just a couple of pipers as expected, but the whole darn band!

For me, personally, it was an emotional moment to see the pipe band weave its way through the revellers. Several years ago I had written to the pipe band asking if they would pipe in the haggis at the inaugural *Mackenzie Muster*. The initial response was they had children in the band, and some parents may not have thought it appropriate. We had come a long way in the last five years.

A moment's (sorry, make that several moments) panic, when we realised the modern sausage style haggis, not at all like the traditional over-filled sheep's stomach, required further cooking. Thank goodness for microwaves.

John McHaffie's stirring address to the now fit for human consumption haggis, captivated the staunch Sassenachs among us. Drawn to highland pipe bands at the tender age of fourteen and continuing to play for the following twenty-five years, yours truly rattled out a suitable percussion accompaniment of flams, drams and paradiddles to the band's medley of tunes, much to the surprise of everyone present, including the band.

A puff of smoke from the boiler in *The Perches*, did not indicate the Pope was dead, but heralded the first stirrings of life next morning. It was almost as though there was a competition as to who could place the first log of wood on the destructor.

Clouds of steam and the sounds of morning ablutions emanated from the shower room. Who were those special people that kept up the supply of hot water and kept everything clean? It just got done, like the myriad of other tasks we were thankful for, during this memorable celebration of naturist life.

Pos Shute headed off challenges from other competitors during the bare buns cross-country race, though not the one he was expecting from across the Tasman. Hard on his heels during the first of the three 2.5km laps was the eventual winner of the children's section.

Nell blitzed the field of women, her winning streak pictured in a two page feature article in the following Saturday's *Timaru Herald*. Runners and walkers alike crossed the finish line, several with grim determination written all over their faces; others laughing with the fun of it all.

Stanton, veteran musterer and clad in yellow wet weather gear, methodically dug a trench around the perimeter of the marquee, creating a diversion over parched Mackenzie tussock. The naked

Top: John McHaffie addresses the haggis; Bottom: Nell Husband blitzed the field of women in the bare buns fun run.

plumber fixed temporary guttering. The storm was nearly over. We were dry. Thanks to a huge gas fan heater, we were warm also.

It was the *Lowland Games* in the marquee and *Brian's Onion Marathon*, that not only brought the most laughs, but tears to the eyes as well. Teams battled it out to peel a bag of onions, ready for the evening barbecue. With many of the Lions Club on grand-parenting duties, cunning deployment of culinary tasks ensured the meal was served hot, on time, and plenty of it.

Lion Brian McNab smothered a laugh as he carefully rearranged Jim's kilt prior to his taking the stage at the *Tartan Tie & Boot Party*. Jim, half of Ashburton duo *No Strings Attached*, thought the flat part went to the back, in order to sit down comfortably. He would have received a sharp reminder, had the kilt pin been in the correct place. Vicki's tartan shawl eventually became a sarong and before you knew it, *No Strings Attached* became *No Clothes Attached*.

Promising to return the following year, these talented musicians were last seen frolicking naked among the lupins for a memorable cover shot.

Our gaggle of golfers, being good sorts, complied readily with the rule of playing naked during the first and last rounds of their chosen 9 or 18 holes, resulting in the trophy being awarded to three winners. Lorna, pan-faced, awarded top marks to the Aussies who played the complete round sans trousers.

During the previous six years, guest nights at *Aoraki Naturally* had increased at a steady rate and although we knew the potential was there to grow the business even more, we were unable to purchase the property. Our efforts to lease on a long term basis, or even a first option to buy, fell on deaf ears.

Even though we had made so many good friends (50% of our visitors were regulars), many of whom had rightly earned their own tangible place at *Aoraki Naturally*, we decided to search for another venue. Whether in the immediate area, or elsewhere, we were determined to continue our work and remain in the South Island. After drawing up a plan which necessitated selling my home in Christchurch, with the flats in Lake Tekapo as collateral, we informed everyone that this was to be the penultimate *Mackenzie Muster*.

The gauntlet was down as we prepared for the final fling. Pos was already in training.

World Naked Bike Ride

Preparation is the key and with this in mind, my new friend, Nell Husband and I, took on the task of promoting this fun event in Lake Tekapo, in the short time available. Hey, what's two weeks in a girl's life?

Our plan was to ride a section of State Highway 8, the Blue Ribbon tourist route, between Christchurch and Queenstown, from our entrance at *Aoraki Naturally*, turning left at the flyover on the Pukaki Canal Road, continuing to *Mount Cook Salmon Farm*, returning the same way. Nell set to and gained permission from *Meridian* who owned the Canal Road, while I telephoned our local Police constable to advise him of our intentions. The response was positive, with *Meridian* confirming within a very short time frame.

Our friendly constable apologised for being unable to be there on the day, as he would be spending the day with his children at the *Weetbix Triathlon*. After asking him for any advice he might have, he responded by suggesting we notify on-coming traffic by way of a simple sign at the front and rear of our group.

We eagerly accepted enough water bottles for our cyclists from Timaru's representative for *Smoke Free*, Leola Ryder, and *Aoraki Organic Co-op* donated a gift basket, with the proviso that Nell advertised their business on her bare back. Several other prizes were produced for the day.

Meantime, back in the office, yours truly, NIFOC (nude in front of computer), put together a web page linked to www.worldnakedbikeride.org and kept in touch with others planning naked bike rides on the same day. Press releases were followed up by the expected flurry of calls from radio and television networks. Our local paper displayed a colourful photo of Kay in training at our scenic grounds, with all the details of the bike ride.

Expecting around a dozen cyclists, by the time we complied with the local constable's suggestion and painted notice boards for the support crew, our cosmopolitan group of sixteen naturists were totally engrossed in organising banners and flags to secure to their bikes, and body paint, advertising our cause.

If ever there was a day for sunshine this had to be it. Our neighbour from *Irishman Creek Station*, Justin Wills, called in with a friend. I jokingly asked if he wanted to borrow a couple of bikes for the naked bike ride. 'No,' was the reply, 'We want to play golf. Any chance of borrowing your golf clubs instead?'

What a special treat then, to be greeted halfway along the canal road by Justin, his wife Gillian, and their friend, with celebratory champagne and crisps. Toots from locals and tourists alike in cars and tour buses with friendly, but surprised Asian tourists waving madly, heralded our progress with many, many photographs taken along the way and again at our destination.

We enjoyed a tail wind on our return journey, but Bernie couldn't wait for the creek and dived into the canal to cool off. Naked riders aged 5 to 65 completed the 28km, with spot prizes prior to a mid-afternoon barbecue.

Free-Wheelers of Lake Tekapo enjoyed a wonderful weekend of camaraderie, with friends all promising to do it all again next year.

From time to time I receive an email from our friends from California still chuckling over their surprising weekend.

And so what was it all about?

Seriously, we face vehicle traffic with our naked bodies as the best way of defending our dignity and exposing the unique dangers faced by cyclists and pedestrians, as well as the negative consequences we all face, due to dependence on oil and other forms of non-renewable energy.

I wonder if anyone noticed the u-turn when the sparkling red Lamborghini turned up at the salmon farm, providing a great photo opportunity, not only for ourselves, but also for the driver, who stripped naked for a celebratory pose.

All Around the UK and More . . .

Seasoned travellers by now, Brian and I were unwilling to spend a long, cold winter in Lake Tekapo. Several of our guests had implored with us to stay longer in the UK and our decision to fly direct to London via Hong Kong seemed the best option. Our stay at Roger and Vena's home in Eltham was always something to look forward to; Roger was a mine of knowledge and extremely helpful regarding the application of computer software; and Vena, a great cook, ran their household with military precision.

Having entertained and fed us well, Roger deposited us at the railway station on time for the long (and expensive) train trip to Liverpool. Ah, but we had our tent, so were economising in other areas – until Brian opened everything up and realised he had left the poles in the wardrobe at home. Luckily for us, a very kind person at *Liverpool Sun & Air* allowed us to stay in their cottage for a few days.

Chester has a delightful mix of Victorian, Gothic and modern styles and was easily reached by public transport. Further exploration around the well preserved docklands at Liverpool more than filled in another day's excursion before our next adventure – across the Irish Sea.

We were assured by Des and Dot, who had visited us several times at *Aoraki*, we would find plenty to see and do on the Isle of Man. Crossing by ferry was surprisingly quick, our arrival coinciding with a beautiful day and during the hair-raising drive up to their beautiful home, we stopped off for a naked sunbathe up in the hills.

And we were busy. Riding on a horse-drawn tram in Douglas, we then took the little steam train to Ramsay and back. We visited the famous *Laxey Wheel* by electric tram, the next leg ferrying us to the top of Snaefell, at 2036 ft, the highest peak on the Isle of Man. Des and Dot treated us royally and were great company, as were all the people who looked after us. Brian would visit them again some years later, to experience what the Isle of Man is world famous for – *The International TT (Tourist Trophy)*

Race; a prestigious motorcycle racing event on a 37 mile course with never ending twists and turns at speeds approaching 200mph.

There were some tense moments (and terse words) as I was forced to relinquish my newly acquired laptop to the luggage section on the returning ferry; even more before we found the coach that was to take us to London. A few deep breaths and we settled back in comfort to take in the scenic English countryside.

Jammed in five o'clock traffic, impatiently eyeballing shop verandas and statues, we inched towards *Victoria Station* and with only moments to spare, laden with baggage, ran blindly to what we hoped was the connecting coach to Norwich.

During their visit to New Zealand in March, Peter and Linda had invited us to stay at their private residence at *Merryhill Leisure* in Norwich. *Deakan Lodge* was no ordinary *'Tingdene'* (park home). More like a swanky apartment, with every imaginable appointment inside, it boasted an outdoor spa which was put to great use by their many friends. Great party animals (one of the owners, Alan Avery has his own dance band), the *Merrymakers of Merryhill* had organised a *'black & white'* themed party. Now with a Kiwi connection, the *'All Blacks'* were deservedly judged best group table.

All too soon our sojourn in the UK concluded and the Netherlands beckoned. But on returning to Eltham, we received the news that Marcella had 'flown the coop', taking the children with her! Brian and I made up our minds right there on the spot. Our friends at *L'Eglantiere* needed our help; the sooner the better. We immediately changed our plans and purchased a cheap fare with Ryan Air to Pau where we were greeted by a distraught, yet somewhat relieved, Xavier Feraut.

Understandably, the weeks that followed at *L'Eglantiere* were tense and, as often happens in these situations, long discussions into the night ensued. But we had work to do and Dutch families were arriving in droves for their holidays during the next few months.

If I was lucky, I could get my daily 'K' in the pool around 7:00am before counting bread, croissants and chocolate au pain and then bringing all the fruit and vegetables out from the large outdoor cooler into the shop, first thing every morning. It was a hectic season and we considered ourselves pretty fortunate when Xavier suggested we make the most of a few days at *Arnachout*, a naturist village of 45 hectares, spreading onto the Atlantic Coast. It was relatively quiet while we were there, but we still enjoyed much of the local cuisine and gambolled in the ocean. What was a novelty for me in July was to lie on the beach and call my daughter back in New Zealand on my cell phone, only to learn she was partying with my sister Sue, who was celebrating her big 60!

Refreshed, we helped out at *L'Eglantiere* for a few more weeks before exploring Aveyron again with its many beautiful castles and famous *Roquefort* cheese. We were keen to drive over the Millau viaduct, which we had learnt about during a previous visit to the area. A quick map reference revealed Millau to be just over an hour's drive from *Village du Bosc*, a family owned campsite of 25 acres of land within a naturist zone of 200 acres, much of it a dark red ochre. The campsite overlooked Lake Salagou, a listed site where it was possible to swim in its many creeks, also wind-surfing, fishing and other water sports. We stayed in one of many unusual hexagonal shaped hinged wooden cabins, which looked as though you could dismantle them easily by just loosening a few bolts.

Nowadays we can turn to the Internet for several reviews, but word of mouth is always the best referral of all. Which was how we heard about *Lissart*; a tranquil spot situated in the Tarn region near Cordes. As with most French naturist sites *Lissart* had a large swimming pool. The bar was unique in that it worked on an honesty basis. Bread could be ordered in high season and pizzas ordered once a week. We made the most of the mobile crepe vendor who also called in weekly and also joined in one of their collective barbecue evenings. This was one of the few French sites where it was possible to walk to the local village. Sadly, Lissart will remain closed to the public as the owners found it too much work and too expensive to keep operating.

San Francisco beckoned, with friends Janie and Jim, who had invited us to stay with them for a few days. Since taking up residence in Lake Tekapo and my increasing use of the Internet, I had taken an interest in *Lupin Naturist Club* located in nearby Silicon Valley and communicated with the manager; initially because of the wild flowers of the same name growing so profusely in the Mackenzie country. A short break to stay with Paul and Diana there, was arranged as well. *Lupin* had been going through some difficult ownership problems at the time, resulting in a neglected appearance. Thankfully this matter has been rectified, with Lupin again recognised as one of California's more popular naturist resorts.

Later, keen to explore further with Janie and Jim, we learned a great deal about the San Francisco area; the devastating 1906 earthquake and the resulting rebuild, its iconic winding roads, Alkatraz Island and of course, the Golden Gate Bridge.

Janie and Jim were great hosts and we couldn't get enough of downtown San Francisco, which seemed to adopt a new culture each day. Exploring on our own we took an exciting ride on the world famous cable car, then found a great restaurant with a bar which seemingly went on forever, attended by impeccably dressed waiters. A couple of places quickly came available and we were ushered on to bar stools with a flourish. Further flourishes as orders taken for food and wine followed and as expected, beautiful cuisine. We excitedly regaled to our hosts, our 'find'.

'Oh goodness,' remarked Jim, 'you normally have to queue for at least an hour there, it's so popular.'

Although most of New Zealand was basking in the warmth of spring by our return in mid-September, it was a somewhat chilly welcome in Lake Tekapo. Our resolve to relocate was even stronger and we spent hours and hours researching and viewing likely locations.

Unable to find a suitable property within the Canterbury or Central Otago area, we turned our attention to the top of the south, to Marlborough. However, it was becoming evident that there were many real estate agents who had no idea of the meaning of the word private and to a large extent, they were no different in Marlborough either!

Eagle-eyed Brian spotted the poster in the Blenheim window and closer inspection revealed a 2.5 hectare property in Wairau Valley, about 30 minutes drive from Blenheim. The tree-lined drive held great appeal, as did the garden and orchard toward the rear. It was obvious the large home was of modern construction and up for auction.

When could we see it? We only had a couple of days in which to view and gratefully made an appointment for later in the afternoon. In our view, the property met all our requirements, although we realised there was a great deal of work to be done plus the ongoing maintenance on such a large established garden. Our biggest problem was that we had not sold either of our own properties, Brian's block of flats in Lake Tekapo, or my house in Christchurch. Consequently, we were not in a position financially to place a bid. Turning our attention to my house in Christchurch, this was quickly prepared for sale and just as quickly realised a buyer.

By this time, it was November 2005. Armed with our business plan and with suitable finance arranged, we drove the eight hour journey to Blenheim again, only to find the photo had been removed from the window. Curious, Brian ventured inside to enquire what figure the property fetched at auction, only to learn it had not receive a bid! Barely containing our excitement – and

All Around the UK and More . . .

Clockwise from top left: The Laxey Wheel on the Isle of Man; All Blacks table at Merryhill Leisure Club; Brian on the beach at Arnachout; Milau Bridge; Kay in the bar at Lissart; Our delicious seafood platter at Arnachout; Kay calling home on the beach.

once we had satisfied ourselves with the documentation at the *Marlborough District Council* – made an offer which predictably, was met with a considerably higher counter offer, we drove home.

I was mindful of the old adage learnt years ago that whether buying or selling, the first one who speaks loses. After rattling the petty cash tin, we zipped our lips and continued with our plans for 'the final fling' at *Aoraki* and, unwilling to break the pattern of the past five years, to visit Europe again in the winter.

The tree-lined driveway of what was to be our new home in Wairau Valley.

The Final Fling

If journalists were to enquire of several participants, 'What was the highlight during the *Mackenzie Muster* this year?' They would receive a similar number of responses.

For me, it had to be the arrival of the *Mackenzie Highland Pipe Band* during the *Gathering of the Clans*. Okay, they were a drummer short, and my apprehension at being invited to accompany the band was quickly dispelled, once I had rattled out a few flams and drags. What great fun, as were the many encores, as were the ageing Highland dancers atop tables.

Due to illness, our regular entertainer, *Switched-on*, Tony Wheeler, was unable to join us for the final fling. Consequently we had to make some rapid changes to Friday evening's program. *Dot's Lot* brought a special 'guest' all the way from Memphis to celebrate 50 years of Rock 'n Roll, then kept us all happy with great disco music from the right decades, too! The sight of Dot's vertically challenged and rather rotund figure squeezed into a gorgeous white and beaded Elvis costume, complete with dark wig and sideburns (sorry to roll out this tired old cliché), but . . . you had to be there!

'Stick to the knitting,' was the catchphrase with the annual naturist festival and this one was to be no exception.

Pos blitzed the field for the second year running, winning the cross-country fun run with the added comment that 'the Aussie never showed up again'. There were some terrific finishes, walkers and runners alike, especially from the youngest of them all.

Pos Shute, second time winner of the Mackenzie Bares Cross-Country Fun Run Trophy.

Clockwise from top: Nude mountain bike race; Mackenzie Highland Pipe Band; Nick Lowe breaches Irishman Creek; Touring B&B Company; Nude Golf International at the Balmoral Golf Course; Members of the Lake Tekapo Lions Club.

THE FINAL FLING

The Press photographer arrived in time for the mountain bike race, to snap a very sedate tandem couple from the UK pictured in Monday's morning paper, quite a different scene from the fast-paced heats run in and around the campsite and egged on by a vocal crowd. Each competitor was presented with their own personal bicycle condom for seat hygiene (amazing what uses we find for plastic food covers).

Did someone mention food? It was breakfast time and the Naked Chef again cooked up a storm.

Stanton picked up where he left off last year, one more time around the marquee in case we had a storm, and of course we didn't. Okay, there might have been a bit of a wind from time to time, but the pictures told the story of the weather on the day, every day. Mostly fine.

More food, as members of the *Lake Tekapo Lions Club* dished up a superb barbecue meal; on time, hot, and plenty of it.

No Strings Attached got the crowd going again on Saturday night's *Tartan Tie & Boot Party* and again morphed into *No Clothes Attached*. What great entertainers! What a magnificent tartan arrangement!

The scenic course of the *Mackenzie Golf Club* - venue for the nude golf tournament, with twenty-six competitors playing in the buff or was that rough? Roger Finnie repeated his 2004 round, winning the magnificent trophy a second time.

On both Sunday and Monday, teams of naked riders on horseback rode at a sedate pace around the shores of Lake Tekapo, guided by *Mackenzie Alpine Horse Trekking*, much to the surprise of several heavily clad pedestrians.

For the rest of us, a quiet day with not even the energy for a game of Petanque. Some went walking to the tarns, others just yarned and yawned.

Compere for the evening, Bevan, told his peanut butter joke, sorting through a veritable kitchen drawer to remove what was on the woof ov 'is mouf. But it was Amy who stole the limelight. The expression on her face when Bevan picked up the carving knife . . .

This year, top lip sync winners outdid even their previous year's top performance of the *Nude Macarena* with their rendition of *Hanging Bananas*.

To say thank you is just not enough, as we gratefully acknowledge the myriad of businesses and community personnel who contributed sponsorship and prizes to this wonderfully unique event. With special thanks to the many naturist businesses here in New Zealand and overseas that have supported us during the six years we have held the muster.

The film crew of *My House, My Castle* filming a shot on Irishman Creek.

But the applause must go to our musterers without whom there would be no excuse to have had all that fun.

One would be forgiven for thinking that during the previous seven years, Kay and Brian had received their fair share of publicity in Lake Tekapo. Hot on the heels of the final fling, Brian and I were invited to take part in *My House, My Castle*, a television show in which a couple who have radically changed their lifestyle, are filmed, providing a marvellous opportunity to promote not only a successful naturist tourism business, but an enjoyable, stress free way of living.

The producer was intrigued about this couple who operate an accommodation venue in the nude for the nude. In our minds we were going about our normal day to day activities; gardening, cleaning etc. However if it gave others some insight into our preferred lifestyle, we were more than happy for TV2 to broadcast the program. No sooner had it finished, than the telephone rang with an enquiry, with a flurry of emails to follow.

A number of weeks later, we were showing a video recording of the program to a group of southerners up for the weekend. One of the scenes depicted Brian striding down the paddock armed with his shepherd's stick, while Nud bounded over the fences.

'Wayleggo,' cried Brian to Nud, (encouraging Nud to herd the sheep).

'What a lot of bullshit,' emitted a gravelly voice from the South, knowing full well the thirty or so Merinos never required any encouragement to trot up to the fence to see Brian.

We all have to live with discreet camera angles before 8.30pm, and pixilation was not an option by the producer and certainly not from us. We could be thankful for that. We were more than happy with positive feedback from friends, family and especially our new customers.

If that wasn't enough, *Radio New Zealand* broadcasted an interview with Todd Nyall twice in one day. So it was not surprising we continued to welcome an increasing number of visitors during the summer.

The Final Fling

The World Naked Bike Ride was again timed for mid-March. We are pretty keen on bikes and the Free-wheelers of Lake Tekapo were out in force. WNBR was held without incident, along the main highway and scenic canal road along State Highway 8. 'Okay, so it's a protest against oil dependency. Some would say nude living is a form of protest against society?'

Although the Free-wheelers of Lake Tekapo enjoyed only half the distance they covered the previous year, friends from neighbouring farms turned out in support and there were plenty of friendly toots and waves from cars and tourist coaches.

Next on the calendar was the Bunnies and Bares, held . . . yes, you guessed correctly . . . during Easter Weekend, which was more of a farewell party, as we had signed the purchase agreement for our new home in Wairau Valley, to take effect as from 28 September 2006, the day after our return from Europe.

I wrote in our newsletter, 'When you visit us, you can see the care some of the bares have given our grounds, including the track all the way alongside the creek.' Russell, who was responsible for many of the tracks, wrote the final entry in our visitors' book. That 'it was the only day he had not enjoyed himself at *Aoraki*, because it was the last of 115 nights since he and Janis first arrived with their caravan in tow in September 2001.'

Russell Giles with Kay on his last day at *Aoraki Naturally*.

The *South Canterbury Community High Country Herald* front page article, read as follows:

'Tekapo will be 'stripped' of their world-renowned naturist park next week when *Aoraki Naturally* owners, Kay Hannam and Brian Williams, say goodbye to the Mackenzie region.

The passionate pair are packing up and moving to Marlborough to run another naturist park in the Wairau Valley – the couple's ultimate naked ambition.'

Our friends in Lake Tekapo also gave us a great send-off; followed by several days of intensive packing and clearing the site at *Aoraki*, assisted by Lions Club members and friends.

The campsite was stripped of everything that could be removed without the walls falling down, plus underground cables and powered site connections, shower trays, even the kitchen sink.

Tony Nee drove the removal truck not just once, but made the return trip three times, as he and Brian moved all our belongings, which also included four huge Oregon beams, rhubarb plants, salt & pepper and book collections, ancient wooden skis, several pairs of ski-boots, aforementioned flying goggles and stretchers, vintage cameras, cooking utensils, a destructor (chippie heater to southerners), and a family of smurfs. In other words, an assortment of Brian's s***t that he could not bear to be parted from, was squeezed into a large storage shed at our new property.

We then loaded up both car and truck, towing trailers packed to the gunnels, to our overnight stop with Stanton. Yes, it snowed and yes, we were glad to be on the plane again at last.

The high country characters were taking off!

The Bag Boy Goes to Europe

'D'ya take trailer trash?'

Two years prior to our move north, a younger looking guy stepped down from his medium sized truck, introduced himself as Dave Care and with a mischievous grin, signalled his plush looking 5th wheeler hooked on the back. We both instantly took a liking to Dave, the brim of his leather Akubra (Australian slouch hat) meeting Brian's chin. It became apparent Dave Care and TT were here for the long haul, as he soon made himself indispensible around the grounds. We became firm friends and above all, his ability to consume copious amounts of red wine soon rivalled that of Brian's.

Brian and I had completed our travel arrangements to visit France and Spain several months earlier, and it was late one evening (during a chat over a couple of glasses of red wine), when Dave passed a comment regarding what he was going to do with himself over the winter, especially now we were moving north.

'Oh for goodness sake,' I remonstrated. 'Stop procrastinating. Why don't you carry our bags and come to Europe with us? You'll find plenty to do at *L'Eglantiere*. Get on the internet and organise your flight.'

I went to bed and left them to continue their deliberations.

'Do you think Kay really meant it?' Dave's concern was genuine.

'Believe me,' said Brian. 'Kay wouldn't suggest it if she didn't mean it'.

Brian and I had decided to bite the bullet and fly Premium Economy. Luckily, Dave managed to secure a return ticket on the same flight and the three of us met at *Auckland International Airport*. As is per usual, Premium Economy passengers were called to join those first on. On hearing the call, Dave jumped up and picked up our bags, depositing them at the gate.

'There you are, Sir. There you are, Madam.'

Still laughing, indulging in the luxury of comfortable spacious seats and extra leg room upstairs, Brian and I slurped on a complimentary glass of bubbles. Mindful of his friend below, Brian popped down, picking up a Moro bar from the basket on the way.

'There you are, my good man,' chipped Brian, 'that's for carrying our bags'.

'Oh, Master, you are so kind.' was the cheeky reply.

Later, during the long haul flight, Brian descended a second time to have a chat with his friend, only to find him armed with a bottle of bubbly, with a grin from ear to ear.

Curious, Brian naturally wanted to know how he managed to score a full bottle of wine. Apparently the flight attendant had overheard their earlier conversation, whereupon Dave told her, 'My owners are upstairs and as I'm only the bag boy, I have to stay down here in cattle class.'

In London, *Eltham Palace* provided a touch of *Art Deco* of historical relevance, and was well worth a visit. Next on our list was *London Imperial War Museum*, but the *Maritime Museum* was more to my liking. A spin on the *London Eye* gave us a bird's eye view of the city. Other London highlights included *Trafalgar Square*, where the fourth plinth boasted a statue of a naked, pregnant, Alison Lapper, with no arms, in stark contrast to the equestrian statues of British Empire heroes.

Lunch with my niece Mhairi (at that time living and working in London) at *The Camel & Artichoke*, concluded a fast paced comprehensive tour of the city. Roger and Vena had made arrangements for us to travel south for a short naturist holiday.

First stop, *South Hants Country Club*, with rows of mobil-homes and caravans, bordered with little ingenuity and dwarfed by the electricity pylons above. Coming from New Zealand with lovingly cared for surroundings; it was hard to believe this was a naturist club. Its saving grace – an indoor heated swimming pool – and the interior of our accommodation was perfect!

Marc Quinn's Alison Lapper Pregnant on Trafalgar Square's fourth plinth.

On the return journey, a visit to Portsmouth satisfied my affinity with the sea, as I stood in awe of *HMS Victory* and absorbed 800 years of naval history.

Life was pretty busy at *L'Eglantiere* where Brian and I and the bag boy kick-started our summer in France together by helping on this lovely campsite in the Pyrenees, catering to mostly Dutch and French naturists. Armed with a chainsaw, the bag boy took on the mantle of *Coupe d'abor*, making short shrift of large over-grown trees around the 43 hectare campsite. Slipping off safety gear for wetsuit, Dave soon had the attention of a group of youngsters keen to master the technique required for canoeing down the River Ger.

Dave instructs a young group safe techniques in canoeing.

Visiting Brits were immediately hit on to exchange reading material. As per usual we met many folk interested in travelling to New Zealand, surprised at meeting Kiwis on a French campsite, but eager to receive information and advice for their visit to our country. It was also fun to meet up with friends Noel and Shona Thomas, on holiday in Europe. We decided to have a Kiwi evening and the young animations director, Chloe (all five foot nothing), swotted up the haka on google, intent on instructing the many Dutch visitors after dinner. Our visitors quickly got into the spirit of things, animating Chloe's fierce expressions.

Personnel helping at the campsite included Dutch and French of varying ages, also a British girl resident in a nearby village, commuting on a daily basis to help in the snack bar. The new French chef served a wonderful variety of meals in the evenings with Demi-Chef, Brian, providing lunch for personnel and visitors. We were now well entrenched into the French way of life, with Dave well ahead with the French language. While I endeavoured to give it my best shot, it's a toss up between Brian and Dave as to who is ahead on red wine.

Bastille Day; celebrated in France on 14 July and at *L'Eglantiere*, the celebrations were no less traditional if a little different. Xavier and the children decorated the golf-cart with tri-colour sun umbrellas and laden with copious amounts of salami, cheese, bread and wine, the entourage of family and personnel toured the campsite, accompanied by unmistakable French music and songs.

A short drive in several directions took us to some of the most beautiful countryside in France, much of which is included in the *Tour de France* cycle race. Side trips included a visit to our old friend Jan Pasma at *Le Vallon des Oiseaux* in Provence and a return visit to *Lissart* in the Averyon region, followed by a week on the Mediterranean.

There are many resorts in Europe that feature a well appointed naturist campsite with an adjoining beach used exclusively by naturists. One of the best is *La Grand Cosse* set in a superb natural location, with direct private access to a 2km long naturist beach.

Situated halfway between Beziers and Narbonne, the campsite blends beautifully with natural surroundings; on one side the Mediterranean Sea and on the other, the vines, lakes and dramatic landscape of the Massif de la Clape.

Within an hour's drive is the walled town of Carcassone; the picturesque Canal du Midi and closer still, the stunning coastal village of Gruissan.

This was our second visit to *La Grande Cosse* and we were again pleased to note none of the usual clothing restrictions applied in their busy reception area. Judging by the friendly hum, the staff were able to converse in English, Dutch, German as well as Spanish.

Instead of pitching our tent as was the case three years previously, Brian and I, together with the bag boy, opted for a week in one of the newly constructed two bedroom chalets. We had been helping at *L'Eglantiere* for the past eight weeks and we were ready to be spoilt. We were not disappointed. Our accommodation was well appointed, with hot shower and toilet.

The campsite is well designed, yet has a casual beachy feel. The one way alpha numero road map provided with a comprehensive brochure of the resort, relieved the frustration of finding our site in such a large complex. In two shakes of a lamb's tail we had our Peugeot parked alongside and began unloading our gear.

We exchanged greetings with our Belgian neighbours through the wild azaleas which separated each site. Dense Eucalypts screened our back door, so we could only hear the seemingly large Spanish family tucked into a caravan. Before long we had stocked up the fridge, tossed our duvets on the beds and were under the gazebo thoughtfully provided over the outdoor furniture. Glass of van rouge at hand, we waded into our treat for the day: cherries and chocolate mouse (the bag boy's favourite). After all, this was the South of France, and we were on holiday.

Clockwise from top right: Remi board-surfing on the River Ger; Totem pole by the river; Brian all decked out for Bastille Day celebrations; The Tour de France zips through nearby Lannemezzan; Sculpture at the Pic du Midi; Young French personnel at L'Eglantiere.

Top: Kay returning via the beach at La Grand Cosse from the nearby village of St Piere sur mer; Bottom: Dave makes the most of a plate of cherries.

Making our way through the sealed cycle/walkway from our location in Row T, we noted several well-appointed Sanitaires; well designed for all abilities and meticulously tiled. I lost count of the showers, toilets, handbasins and washing up areas. Each complex was colourfully identified with decorative tiles. No fear of getting lost here.

Chien is French for dog and there was even an outside bath and shower for the little critters. Thankfully, there was no other 'evidence' of our canine visitors.

Over to one side of the campsite I spotted the gymnasium mentioned in their brochure. Strewth! We were getting enough exercise finding our way down to the bar! There also seemed to be quite a lot of activity in the building alongside, with the ankle-biters hard at it constructing crafts of some sort.

Ah, the swimming pools. Recent improvements gave the whole pool area an inviting tropical ambience. Sensible footwear storage and shower located immediately inside the entrance, ensured the clean and well cared for surroundings remained in the same fashion.

Thankfully, the larger pool was less crowded than expected and I emerged 45 minutes later brimming with smug satisfaction.

Time to hit the beach!

Ten minutes later we were all decked out with sun umbrella, rugs, and cold drinks, soaking up the last of the afternoon's rays. All the stories you have heard about the Med' are true. It is an incredible shade of blue. Yes, you do float; and it is so warm. Oh, and a big plus, the lovely sandy beach is groomed every day.

Back home in New Zealand we are constantly reminded to keep out of the sun. Here in France we safely toasted a golden hue, the envy of my kiwi friends.

Later in the week we three made a concerted effort to do some exercise, strolling along the full length of the naturist section before slipping on a sarong ten minutes prior to arriving at the burgeoning village of St Piere sur mer. Saturday's market was in full swing, offering curtain-hooks to handbags plus all manner of local produce, reasonably priced too!

Lunch was special, provided by a typical family operated, mobile pizza kitchen, where you could view the patriarch creating your own personal pizza whilst chatting to you from his work table. Mama and all the young adult children were engaged in either food preparation, cleaning up or taking orders. The result was divine!

La Grande Cosse had a pretty good social atmosphere around the bar and restaurant. *World Cup Football* had taken over and of course we were caught up with the parochial cheering from Italian, Dutch and German supporters.

Wasn't it nice the owners remembered us from last time? Taking time out to say farewell, presenting us once more with a complimentary bottle of the region's van rouge. Now all we needed were the cherries and a plate of chocolate mouse for the bag boy.

In Spain, we pitched our tents and lazed on the beach at *El Templo del Sol* for a few days, with a side trip to Barcelona, before heading south to *El Portus*, a beautiful naturist resort near Cartegena in Spain, where I was to attend the INF Congress as NZNF Delegate. From an initial reading of the twenty-three page agenda it appeared we would have a packed weekend.

El Portus Naturist Resort, Spain.

Spanish Hospitality

We, including the bag boy, who had seemingly morphed into the NZNF Security Advisor, had a busy weekend.

'Security advisor?' I hear you cry.

After seeing Dave in the rear vision mirror, with wrap around shades and walkman plugged in for good effect, we knew Dave took his job really seriously, to the extent he even took to sleeping outside on the balcony. His diligence in screening local wine and beer should also not go un-noticed.

Roz, the other half of Mick Ayers from the INF Committee, was quite sceptical of Dave's new found status until she saw his sleeping bag laid outside the door of our cabin.

This was the fourth INF Congress I had attended and was certainly the most intensive, with professional presentations and workshops on the new INF-FNI politics, together with the adoption of a Naturist Accreditation procedure.

The Congress was originally planned for at *Costa Natura* where, due to new management, they were unable to fulfil these obligations, hence the change of venue. 25 delegates took part in the congress, together with members of the INF Executive Committee.

Three translators worked under sweatshop conditions for several hours each day to ensure everyone understood each other.

Anyone who thinks that involvement in the INF Congress

The 60th INF World Congress at *El Portus,* Spain.

is nothing but a free lunch, can think again. Despite four days of meetings, workshops, emotive displays of criticism, difficulties with translation, not to mention the temperature of the room at times well into the 30's, I felt this year's Congress was a much more progressive event, with a great deal to look forward to. Yes, the lunch was free, as was the superb hospitality of the *Spanish Naturist Federation*. The Congress banquet, held at a posh restaurant in Cartagena attended and funded by local tourism officials, was like nothing ever before.

In his report, President Wolfgang reported the first of the proposals to bring the INF ship back on course with projects such as naturist certification, naturist database and new INF policies. The INF took part in a hearing in Rome, at which MPs of various parties were informed by naturist organisations, about how positive naturism can be for society. The bill on the recognition of naturism is currently going through parliament in Italy.

Vice President, Charles Obergfell, had previously participated in several meetings, including developing countries Romania, Brazil and Argentina, as well as other European organisations. His introductory topic, A worldwide friendship chain, referred to the common points in naturism. In contrast, the co-theme, The naturist revolution, from Ishmael Rodrigo, President of the Spanish Federation, stressed the right to be naked. Both speeches highlighted the values of our international network.

When visiting naturist sites around Europe, it's not often you are given the opportunity to become acquainted with the owners. As we ourselves well know, they are usually looking after all their guests' requirements and don't often take time out for themselves, let alone satisfy the curiosity of three itinerant kiwis.

Carmen and Diego, owners of *Sierra Natura Naturist Resort* in Spain, are the exception. In an endeavour to capture their life story, I understood many of the attributes which make this couple so interesting and why they and *Sierra Natura* enjoy a special place in the hearts of many of their visitors.

As with many places we visited during our travels in Europe, word of mouth brought us to the impressive entrance. The unusually artistic cement and steel gate silently glided across the driveway, automatically closing behind our little Peugeot.

Although we had seen photos of the buildings in the Dutch *Naturisme* magazine, it was nothing compared to the actual view of the Cupola, the main building, housing reception, shop, kitchen, restaurant, library and communal lounge. This large, seemingly haphazardly constructed concrete building, has not a straight line in sight. A number of skylights in the concave roof and large east-facing windows with curved framing, created a wonderful kaleidoscope of colour and light inside. Further inspection outside, revealed several buildings with the same theme.

'Bedrock,' said Brian. Not unkindly, I hasten to add.

'So where does Diego get all his ideas from?' I enquired, as I looked around the buildings which rather resembled giant concrete mushrooms, a curious blend of Gaudi and the Flintstones.

'He just fantasizes and dreams a lot,' Carmen smiled. 'He doesn't like symmetric design. In fact he's never had any formal training in design at all'.

The building we parked outside, used to house animals before Diego transformed it into a communal lodge, complete with large dining/living; a kitchen with no less than four refrigerators; two large bathrooms and four bedrooms. We had stayed in a variety of accommodation and had to admit, king-size bunks were a first!

On to an inspection of smaller units and the artistic flair of the owner was prevalent here also, with leafy designs on moulded concrete and mesh structures. Fascinating!

Diego had first worked as general dog's-body in a nudist campsite in Corsica before he met Carmen in 1980. A surprise for me was Carmen's fluency in English, having spent ten years in Australia with her family, before Papa insisted they all return to Spain in the hope his daughters would marry Spanish people. Neither he nor Carmen were to be disappointed. A few years later she met Diego, and Carmen was to experience her first holiday with the freedom from clothes at *Las Palmeras* in Vera.

'I was very shy,' she confided. 'I thought everybody was going to look at me. Right away, I realized of course, that no-one was looking. Now, whenever we are deciding on a vacation each winter, we always choose a natural place, *Cabo de Gata* in Almeria being the most favoured. It's not naturist, but you can go natural if you want.'

Those initial years were a difficult time for the young couple, torn between living in the city with a greater chance of making an income, or, starting from scratch in rugged countryside near Alicante, originally hand terraced in the early days for olive trees and wheat.

Diego's brother was already in the process of establishing a large textile accommodation and camping facility, complete with restaurant in an adjoining property. Carmen chose the countryside and was chef for many years next door, while Diego created their very own dream *Sierra Natura*.

Carmen and Diego now have two grown daughters of their own. One makes goats cheese in Barcelona, while the other works full time at the campsite. It is hard work for the family and doesn't stop in the winter, as Diego and his family and friends continue to work on their latest project. Carmen manages to take time out for herself, but is also busy making preserves from their extensive garden.

After almost thirty years of work in progress, *Sierra Natura* boasts a spacious camping ground in a completely natural setting, with several electric hook-ups and tent sites; car park; a variety of accommodation, some of which is self-contained; sauna, above which is a sunbathing area and the most natural looking (and feeling), solar-heated swimming pool you could ever imagine, complete with water-slide, outdoor shower and children's pool. A Jacuzzi will be in operation the following season.

We were into day three of a very relaxing holiday, with swimming and sunning high on our list of priorities. Reluctantly extricating ourselves from our deck chairs, we found ourselves at the summit of one of the walking trails in and around the campsite.

The surrounding countryside has many features and we were privileged to spend a morning with the area manager of the Department of Tourism, exploring ancient rock drawings which have been preserved with secure barriers to prevent them being vandalized. This area has become quite a focal point for visitors, especially those interested in Anthropology.

The final evening of our now week-long stay culminated in a delicious meal for the remaining visitors on the grounds, prepared

SPANISH HOSPITALITY

Clockwise from top right: Kay and Brian by the pool; The Cupola, restaurant and communal lounge; Interior view of our accommodation, showing kitchen and dining area; Kay at the door of the Sauna; Carmen and Diego, owners of Sierra Natura;

by the Catalan Chef, Jesus, who, for the past seven years has cooked anything Carmen suggested or that you asked for. Diego ceremoniously opened several bottles of specially prepared champagne (produced by friends and family each year from local grapes). We also sampled a Muscatel which set our palates ready for the feast. To cap it off, we were presented with a bottle of champagne and cask of Muscatel to take back to New Zealand and use to celebrate my 60th birthday.

Spanish hospitality at it's best!

Derek and Judy Christy from Australia, celebrate with Brian and Kay at *Wai-natur*.

Life in the Valley

One would be excused for thinking that life in the valley would move at a slow tempo.

Hah!

Having arrived off the plane and with car, truck and trailers already loaded to the gunnels and waiting for us at Stanton's home in West Melton, an overnight stop at Cheviot seemed the most sensible thing to do before picking up the key to our new home, tackling the task of removing our furniture from the shed into the empty house and making a start on the on-going grounds maintenance.

Knowing the ground in Wairau Valley would be just as hard and stony as at Lake Tekapo, the local digger was contracted to assist Brian and Dave install the underground wiring and powered sites. Within pretty short order they had moved on to the next stage of converting what was a large kennel for the previous owners' five dogs into The Perches. We had brought *The Perches* sign from the old chook house at *Aoraki* and ceremoniously installed it in place. The whelping kennel became a toilet and with the addition of a couple of walls and a sliding door, a shower room completed the project. At a later stage, this area was spruced up even more with floor tiles and facilities for the disabled. Visitors would discern celestial bodies while relaxing in the adjacent garden spa, or keep up their fitness on several items of equipment available. Recently a sauna replaced the fitness centre and completed this popular area.

Complete with wide sweeping verandas, our new home has two guest rooms, both with sliding glass doors opening onto the garden, plus a super-sized guest bathroom. The reception area at the entrance to the house is approached beneath a canopy of magnificent oak and larch trees.

Wai-natur has been promoted as a place where you truly come as you are. Situated in well established, beautiful gardens, it ticks all the boxes for an accommodation venue. There is space and privacy in which to provide camping, with powered and non-powered campsites in the orchard; original buildings have been converted into a communal recreation room with kitchen/lounge and log burner and ablution blocks. Guests can enjoy the intimacy of their own ensuite cabin or shady on-site caravan. With communal barbecue, sauna and garden spa; Wai-natur has all the amenities of a regular camping ground.

Changing location meant changing content throughout our website and promotional material, also. It was quite a marathon, but before long, viewers began checking out the new colours and photos of our lovely new home and its fabulous gardens and *Wai-natur* opened to the public in October 2006.

Of course none of this would have been possible if Brian, doggedly approaching his 70th birthday and the younger, bag boy, had not worked their butts off, ticking off the never-ending items on 'the list'.

Maintenance around the large garden was on-going, but a pattern soon emerged. Although we had brought with us our own ride-on mower, we found another essential item in the shed – a mulcher. It soon became evident as to why it was left behind and a new motor was duly fitted.

With the acquisition of the neighbours' log-burner, and with plenty of TLC, the storage shed had been converted into a cosy rec' room. Recently, we gratefully accepted our new neighbours' old kitchen hardware. Now, with more bench space and cupboard doors of a similar type, the rec' room had become a comfortable living area.

A further caravan was added to our 'fleet' of onsite vans. A couple of portacoms were relocated and refurbished and have been transformed into a comfortable ensuite cabin and a sanitaire.

The installation of a 12 metre solar heated swimming pool was a great attraction, and not just for our guests. I could continue to keep fit, swimming naked in this fabulous salt-water chlorinated pool.

However, the downturn in the European market and the high New Zealand dollar has impacted heavily on the number of overseas visitors. The devastating Christchurch earthquakes eroded a large client base and we are mindful several of our friends continue to live under extremely stressful conditions as they endure the ongoing saga of EQC and insurance companies' protracted settlements.

Up Tempo

Writing had become more than just a hobby for me and I was keen to see our experiences in print. With the bonus of a keen photographer at my side, opportunities to write about our new naturist park and travels to Europe increased, with *gonatural* and other overseas naturist publications eagerly accepting our contributions.

We had plenty to do now we had re-located to Wairau Valley, so I was stunned when Brian telephoned from Auckland where he was attending the NZNF Council AGM just after Christmas. The incumbent editor of *gonatural* magazine, Conrad Inskip, was seriously ill and Brian had suggested to the delegates I take over the job.

Talk about a big mouth! In spite of investing time and effort, not to mention most of our capital, in our new venture, here was Brian prepared to stick his neck out and support me again. I had also heard rumours of the quarterly magazine, which began as an eight page publication in 1956 published by the NZNF, being handed on a plate, so to speak, to one of our competitors. That alone was a good enough motivation for me to accept the challenge of producing our national magazine on behalf of our own organisation.

A few days later I was in Auckland myself, staying with a former editor, Les Olsen and his wife, Laurel, getting a few tips on preparing the magazine for the printer.

Visiting Conrad in hospital, I learned he had done a Polytech course on Adobe InDesign. He not only edited the magazine, but did the design and layout as well. Magazines published during the past two years were kept on the magazine's laptop, with folders containing advertisements, articles and photos. Brian had bitten off some seriously large chunks there.

This was all a bit new to me and I certainly didn't have time to go to Polytech to learn the fundamentals of InDesign. But, after having a quick session with the Auckland printer, I had a more than vague idea of how to go about it. My own experience with MS Publisher helped somewhat, but was nothing compared to the kettle of fish in which I was now completely submerged.

***gonatural* Magazine, Issue #200 March 2007.** A 24 page publication, mostly in black and white, with four colour centre pages and covers, was duly completed and couriered to the printer in Auckland.

Les and Laurel continued distributing personal subscriptions for the next two or three issues, but I was keen to have the magazine printed by a local printer in Blenheim who had offered a considerably cheaper quotation. And so later in the year, Brian and I took over the accounts and distribution of the magazine, with yet another steep learning curve, MS Access, a database which records personal subscriptions.

It made such a difference having the magazine printed locally and distributed from Blenheim. Soon afterwards *gonatural* magazine was increased to 44 pages, all in colour and is currently printed in Dunedin at an even more desirable cost. Distribution continues to be carried out by the printer, with a large consignment forwarded to me to distribute to personal subscribers.

Thanks to a very forward thinking executive and my own attitude of self worth, in September 2009 I entered into a formal contract with the NZNF, and was appointed Managing Editor of *gonatural* magazine. These actions will future proof the magazine's existence and remove the burden of what for many years was largely a volunteer obligation.

There are times when the actual process of putting the magazine together can be a bit daunting, particularly when we have a camp full of visitors and there are a myriad of cleaning and administration tasks to be done. It has been a great deal of fun to have some of our naturist friends around the table, stuffing envelopes on a busy February afternoon. Besides, the bouquets far outweigh the brickbats. But good time and management skills are an essential part of daily life, plus a very understanding partner.

If someone had told me I would not only be editing a magazine one day, but publishing it along with managing the whole shooting box, I would have wondered where they found that idea from.

The tempo was picking up.

Schnappshot of Hungary

For someone who is not fond of travelling, people probably think I'm kidding when I explain my absence from New Zealand for four months during the winter. After all, our summer in France was the sixth time Brian and I closed up shop in May and headed to the warmer climes of Europe.

We had been invited to return to *L'Eglantiere* in the Pyranees. This family owned naturist centre began in the early 70's, set up by Marcelle and Maurice Feraut. Their son Xavier manages the 45 hectare site edged by the River Ger now, with partner Isabelle, and children Iris, Julie, Remi and Suzy; part of our extended naturist family we have become to know and love.

During the first two years, we endured life in a small tent. We were now installed in a veteran on-site caravan acquired for one euro from the previous owner. Meals were to be provided, so our needs other than a bed to sleep in were minimal; a fridge to keep cheese and beer cool; sun umbrella and loungers in the makeshift beer garden; the New Zealand flag hoisted aloft a suitable tree.

Two kiwis – on their honeymoon – arrived in time for the Monday night barbie and were immediately roped in to help. They travelled by train all the way south to nearby Lannemezan to spend time with us and especially enjoyed their tour de France with Brian, taking in the town of La Mongie and the spectacular views from Pic du Midi, 2,854 metres above.

We were also fortunate in having each Sunday free and clocked up many miles in our little Peugeot as we meandered around the surrounding countryside and negotiated narrow roads in quaint towns, petunias and impatiens cascading from every available balcony, bridge and lamppost.

Festivals of all kinds were held during the summer including our favourite, *Jazz at Marciac*, and later in August, a short drive up the hill to Monleon Magnoac and the *Samba Repercussion*.

Summer vacation at *L'Eglantiere* meant there was plenty of entertainment provided for young people: ghost hunting in the forest; raft races and jousting on the swift flowing river being the most favoured by the hordes of young Dutch people.

It was now early September and time for our own short vacation, before flying back home. Family Feraut gave us a special farewell; French champagne with mango icecream before presenting us with a bottle of VSOP Armagnac. (VSOP -very special old product, or is that very special old person?)

Hungary has existed in the centre of Europe for over 1,100 years. Spanning an area of almost 10,000 sq kms, it is bordered by seven countries; yet their language is spoken nowhere else, nor do their folk songs bear any resemblance to those of other nations. With rich wines and thermal spas, Hungary boasts a heritage and cultural diversity that attracts people from far and wide. What makes it even more attractive, it's half the cost.

In Spain the previous year for the INF Congress, we met a number of these warm fun-loving people during a Goulash party put on for the weekend stragglers. As we had planned another trip to Europe, we eagerly accepted an invitation from Dr Janos Sandor, the owner of a naturist campsite near Szeged.

Having worked out the logistics of travelling through South of France, Italy and Slovenia, our arrival coincided with the beginning of *Art Camp*. FKK Camping signs directed us to a rough side road and the entrance to *Sziksosfurdo – Strand Camping*.

'We're nowhere near the beach,' I thought.

In double quick time we were settled into a comfortable caravan, courtesy of Janos, and shed our sweaty clothes. Later, at the snack bar and fast-food restaurant, he introduced us to several professional and amateur photographers and artists, already making the most of the relaxed attitude to photography during the week long *Art Camp*.

Surrounding a large warm lake, *Szikso* covers around two hectares. Since Janos purchased the existing naturist camp three years prior, the vacant land on the other side of the lake has been developed, extending the number of campsites with electric hookups. A huge log cabin has been added which includes a games room, kiddies' corner, sauna and exercise room; it is ideal too, for the art exhibition held at the end of the week.

Birch trees and lovely green lawns provide a natural area around the sandy shore line for artists to display, or create images on canvas. A large section of lake is cordoned off, ensuring a safe area for the ankle-biters; the slide ensures an exhilarating method for kids to get wet. Youth and adults alike make almost continuous use of sporting equipment such as table tennis and volleyball. Such is the popularity of *Szikso*, that on the weekend Hungarian families arrived in droves, with over 400 visitors on site.

A group from the Ukraine had made the challenging journey across to *Szikso*, and we were delighted to renew our acquaintance at the evening barbecue hosted by Janos, with Andrii and his wife Sveta. We also met Mark and Olga and their daughter from Russia; also Solymar from Romania.

A professional masseuse and yoga exponent, Solymar, chatting away to Brian later in the evening, suggested she should pose for him – on top of the pool table!

'Now I wonder where I can get a pool table for home, just like that one,' mused Brian.

An extended invitation was made by a naturist group camped about an hour's drive away alongside the River Tisza. Bearing in mind there would be no facilities, we packed food and drinks. It turned out our preparations were completely unnecessary, as Hungarian hospitality came to the fore again, with hot coffee and Schnapps on our arrival, followed by a delicious soup, hot and spicy; cooked in a large cauldron over the campfire.

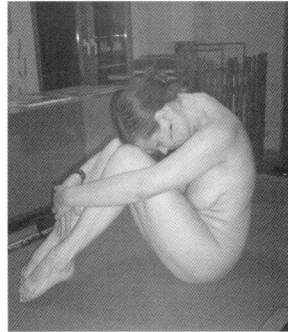

Clockwise from top left: The lake at *Sziksosfurdo*; Solymar strikes a pose on the pool table; Sand sculpture; Artist in residence during *Art Camp* at *Sziksosfurdo*.

Olga sculptured shapes in the sand, others paddled up and down the wide warm river in kayaks or canoes; those who weren't taking photos, just lazed in the shade.

Back at *Szikso*, on the program next day, was body painting and artists excelled with a variety of body art: chains, floral and fauna design, even clothes painted on! With temperatures still in excess of 35 degrees, the real thing was required only much later in the evening.

It was time for us to leave for the next part of our journey; the village of *Balatonbereny*, at the southern end of Lake Balaton, 77kms long by 14kms wide. That's some lake!

Established around the late 1950's, the commercial FKK Camping boasted a large well-manicured campsite with modern facilities, together with a number of chalets for hire. Our accommodation on the other hand, consisted of one of several basic rooms in an old lodge. It was quite adequate, with separate bathrooms, refrigerators in the central hallway, al fresco dining under the porch, and it sure beat putting up the tent!

Access to the lake was by way of steps from a large wooden platform, circular in shape. No jumping into the lake either, as for about 150 metres out it was only waist deep!

After a week of *Art Camp* at *Szikso*, socializing at the bar and restaurant and mingling around the campsite, the early season calm of *Balatonbereny* acquired some adjustment. However all this changed in the weekend, with the arrival of several naturists from a club near Budapest and local members of *Balatonbereny*. Several families were viewed trundling their camp chairs and picnic paraphernalia on small wheeled carts, to establish their patch for the day.

Brian and I were regarded somewhat as mini celebrities and during a 10:00am meeting arranged with the Club President, Tibor Balogh, and other officials, we were introduced to Peter Horvarth, Deputy Mayor of Balatonbereny.

What's the connection? As the village owned the campsite it was in the village interests to support it as 100% of the employees were locals. What made the early morning meeting more surprising, no, make that enjoyable, was the red wine that flowed freely during our discussions about naturism in our respective countries.

During the afternoon Peter escorted us on a tour of the village, where we visited little old cottage museums and saw and learnt a great deal more of the area than we would have otherwise. Later, driving through several vineyards, he showed us the three long rows of grapevines owned by his family, laughingly describing the annual harvest when extended family members turned up to pick the year's harvest, and drink last year's.

Body painting at *Sziksosfurdo*.

The village had several restaurants to choose from, and all were within walking distance. We eagerly sampled some of the local fare, as we liked it hot and spicy. Occasionally we cooked for ourselves, and the local supermarket and fruit & veggie stall supplied all our requirements.

We were directed to *Angela-Farm*, a quiet naturist camp in the middle of nature, surrounded by forests and a lot of sunshine; a wonderful panorama and beautiful location. We took a brief excursion and found a hidden paradise, and Angela herself, who first of all offered us coffee, then a tour of the grounds.

In addition to 25 camp sites we were shown six wooden chalets and three apartments, all well appointed, with everything required for a small house!

Brian tested the 12 x 6 metre swimming pool, albeit briefly and chatted to the only other visitors, a couple from the Netherlands. It was early in the season, although very warm and Angela advised that all the accommodation was booked, and she expected the campsite to be full when the holidays started.

Its location was near the world famous thermal baths of Hévíz, and the coast of Lake Balaton in Keszhely only five minutes away, provided numerous opportunities for our photograph album.

A remarkable occurrence, noted during our travels around the coast of Lake Balaton, and in the thermal towns in particular, were the numbers of Hungarian families, young and old alike, walking about the town in their bathing costumes.

Our sights were on Gardony, a small village handily located to Budapest. Taking the train to visit this huge city seemed the most sensible option and luckily for us, an English speaking student seated alongside provided even more tips regarding transport to view Buda on the west side of the Danube and Pest, the more modern commercial area of the city, on the east.

Trudging up Castle Hill revealed even more history, with the famous *Liberty Statue*, erected firstly in 1947 and commemorating Hungary's liberation from Nazi rule, dominating the skyline.

After all that repression, Hungarians had a lot to smile about now! Our sample of naturism in Hungary might be over for the time being, but unlike the Goulash, we have only had a taste.

Arrivals and Departures

Babies usually arrive when they are good and ready. Only this one needed a little 'hurry up.' Jackie gave birth to Hunter Jai Hart in August 2007, only hours after our arrival back in New Zealand and while driving in the dark to meet the new addition to our family. It was another very emotional time, especially for big brother Will, whom I think was the proudest of us all.

A grandchild fills a space in your heart that you never knew was empty.
Author unknown.

The opportunity to promote New Zealand naturism at a prestigious holiday expo in the Netherlands, came at the invitation of *Internatuur,* a Dutch Naturist Travel company.

I had met the principals of *Internatuur* during the recent INF Congress in Spain and with my knowledge of naturist venues in our country, they were very keen to establish a 'round tour of New Zealand', offering a travel and accommodation package to Dutch naturists. Within a short period of time we had formed a close working relationship, booking accommodation on their behalf with several naturist venues throughout New Zealand.

Having visited the Netherlands on a number of previous occasions, I was familiar with the location: Jaarbeurs Utrecht.

The key consumer and trade show in the Netherlands is *Vakantiebeurs,* to be held in Utrecht from 8–13 January 2008. *Wai-natur Naturist Holidays*, New Zealand exhibited with *Internatuur* (a Dutch Naturist Tour company) on a joint stand within the NFN Naturist Pavilion.

Vakantiebeurs is a six day consumer and trade fair held in the Netherlands annually, with approximately 1500 exhibitors from 150 countries featured in some 11 halls.

Vakantiebeurs 2008 attracted 135,223 visitors – compared to 135,734 in 2007. The difference in the number of visitors was only 0.003% compared to 2007. A survey conducted by the organisers of the event revealed 81% of visitors did so to obtain general information about a vacation and had not yet booked a holiday. Only 3% actually planned to book a vacation on the day they attended.

An increasing number had already chosen their destination before visiting the exhibition, but only booked after gathering detailed information at *Vakantiebeurs*. Asked about the destination for the longest holiday, 51% of visitors opted for Europe, 47% for a faraway destination and 2% for the Netherlands.

The Naturist Pavilion which covered the floor area of a large house had a nautical theme with a central red and white lighthouse, and around the perimeter were 14 stands with displays from several European naturist organisations. The NFN pavilion became alive with body art, sand sculpture, massage, promotion of the Dutch Federation's signature magazine UIT! and a new French naturist magazine, *Let's Go!* In addition, *Internatuur's* stand, which was designed as a beach bar, included our own desk facing the naturist pavilion.

Of the thousands that visited the naturist pavilion, many were pleasantly surprised to find out New Zealand was featured as a destination. Internatuur have included a round trip of New Zealand in their very professional glossy brochure and to have this reinforced by the presence of a New Zealander promoting a variety of naturist accommodation was very much appreciated. I was kept busy responding to questions about all manner of when and where to go.

Kay on the stand at *Vakantiebeurs*.

Visitors to the stand were genuine in their request for information. A continuous laptop presentation featuring naturist venues and scenic areas in New Zealand was greatly admired, as was a display folder containing a similar combination of material. Promotional material was distributed on behalf of *Wai-natur, Pineglades* and *Wellington Naturist Club* and a number of enquiries resulted in sales of *Holidays NZnaturally* and *gonatural* magazines.

Highlights included meeting professionals in the naturist tour business and learning from their experience; forming relationships with other International tour operators and expanding friendships within the European naturist community, in particular the NFN and FENAIT (Italy); advising prospective visitors to New Zealand of naturist accommodation; promoting recognition that New Zealand is part of the naturist global community.

My attendance on the stand spanned 52 hours, breaking for lunch each day and eating 'around the world'. While a good many visited Hall 8 in which the naturist pavilion was situated, it would be fair to say a good majority of visitors made their way to the Canadian and US halls as well. This was understandable, as the US dollar was low at the time, the shorter haul travel much more appealing and the visitor evaluation revealed the Far East and France were the most popular choice of destination.

Aware of how large the *Jaarbeurs* was, nothing really prepared me for the vastness of the interior of the building with its discordant sound and variety of display material of *Vakantiebeurs*. Every holiday product and adventure imaginable was presented. I was among numerous savvy International operators, extremely well funded and displayed accordingly.

It was envisaged by us that the benefits of attending *Vakantiebeurs* would be long term, although I am now reminded the world is gripped by recession and financial controls which have impacted severely on the ability of Europeans to travel long-haul.

There are many Dutch visitors who are plainly unaware that naturism exists in New Zealand. However we need to learn more about our visitors and what they expect to receive when they get here. It is not a case of 'one size fits all'.

Overseas naturists visiting New Zealand do so for a variety of reasons; the naturist ingredient is just part of the experience and what we provide must be of good quality, whether it be sleeping in a tent or campervan; hosted or self-contained accommodation. Information, whether on the Internet or printed brochures, must be presented in a simple, clear format which is easy to comprehend and importantly, reflect the experience on offer.

We have some way to go to match the co-operation and collaboration between naturist centres such as *NatuStar, France 4 Naturisme, Naturisme en Terriors,* even the *Italian Naturist Federation* which comprises commercial sites and to work in a more symbiotic relationship here in New Zealand. The NZNF should encourage similar initiatives.

I recommended that in future, participation at *Vakantiebeurs* may be more cost effective by utilising personal contacts in the Dutch naturist network, who would be willing and capable of representing Naturist Holidays in New Zealand.

Now, the INF offers an opportunity for federations like NZNF to promote their member clubs and organisations at *Vakantiebeurs* and other European holiday fairs, with members of the Central Council freely distributing promotional material.

Wide publicity generated by a media release prior to my leaving, was enough to spark the interest of the *Dominion Post* Tourism Editor, Colin Patterson, who contacted me for an interview while I was at *Rotota* for the National Campout. The subsequent spate of newspaper reports throughout New Zealand, complete with file photos described how, 'one woman's naked ambition to lure more tourists to New Zealand by offering naturist adventures, is taking flight'.

As expected, following another media release on my return, he telephoned for a follow up interview. The resulting article featured in several national dailies. The subsequent interview with Jim Mora on *Radio New Zealand* seemed almost like a reward for visiting the northern hemisphere in the middle of their winter. This type of journalism provides us with the publicity and credibility we so much desire.

The big question is; how can we convince our own freedom lovers in New Zealand who are quite content to relax sans clothing on the beaches and rivers and in their own back yards, to visit clubs and resorts? Rather than bemoaning the decline in members, our own publicity campaigns and marketing here in New Zealand need to be couched in terms that support freedom naturally and body acceptance.

Nude Nuptials

Nude weddings; not a new phenomenon, but we would all like to think our big day would include something rather special to make it unique.

When Des and Dot prepared for their nuptials at *Wai-natur* in February 2008, they were completely unaware of how very special their day was to become.

Des emailed me around mid-June, as he and Dot had stayed at *Aoraki Naturally* on a number of occasions during their travels in New Zealand. Brian and I had also enjoyed their hospitality when invited to stay with them on the Isle of Man a couple of years before, so we had been good mates for some time by now.

We were very comfortable about hosting a nude wedding, having overseen all the finer details of Paul and Diana's marriage at *Aoraki* in December 2001. Although set in somewhat rural simplicity in the Mackenzie, Paul and Diana's big day was celebrated in style with several friends of *Aoraki* and not unwelcome publicity by local media.

I sensed this particular occasion was to be somewhat muted, even though the park-like setting at *Wai-natur* is superb, with five acres of beautiful, established gardens. However, I was not prepared to sacrifice detail and a sense of occasion for these good friends. It could be done tastefully, but without fanfare.

Code name NWODD (Nude Wedding of Des & Dot) was set for 12 noon Sunday 3rd February 2008, during their planned four day stay in our B&B. A friend from Blenheim recommended a local marriage celebrant – John Craighead. Once we had facilitated John's acquaintance with Des and Dot via email, arrangements were made to acquire the marriage licence, and other details were finalised, including the menu for a special luncheon on the day, which would include local seafood and wine from the Marlborough region.

Understandably, this flurry of activity necessitated the bag boy aka the flower boy and Brian grooming our beautiful grounds and, preparing themselves mentally and physically for the task ahead, ie practising the toasts.

All was ready. Des & Dot had arrived at *Wai-natur* a couple of days earlier to meet first of all, the marriage celebrant and to sort out the paperwork. However, John's comment before he took his leave that afternoon, took them by surprise.

'What am I supposed to wear?'

Dot's answer was, 'Whatever you feel comfortable in.'

'Mmmmm. My wife said there is always a first time for everything.'

Which left us all guessing. Will he, or won't he?

A number of casual guests staying on the grounds readily offered their services as rent-a-crowd, providing a welcome addition and adding to the sense of occasion required for the big day. With bubbles chilling and luncheon prepared, the garden setting for the midday nuptials was now basking in sunshine to welcome the marriage celebrant, dressed in sunhat, sunnies and floppy cargo pants.

Not quite what I expected, but after the customary round of handshakes, John's next words were, 'Well, I had better get into the theme of things.'

I quickly led him to one of our guest rooms before he changed his mind. He certainly came out looking as though he had been doing this for ages.

John did not require coercion, or the thought that he might be the odd one out. He just took a commonsense approach which ensured Des & Dot's special day became unique. By divesting himself of clothes, he won a special place in our hearts also.

Following a short and sweet but nevertheless very special, service, our happy couple, having signed the register, were dusted with rose petals by a very attentive flower boy.

The party went on through the afternoon in a slow, slow, quick, quick, slow fashion; dancing on the lawn, enjoying the music, chatting to our friends.

Our retreat later in the evening to the *Wairau Valley Tavern* next door, for a meal and a round or two with rent-a-crowd, capped off a magic, and very unique wedding day.

While Brian was keen to travel during our winter and continue helping at *L'Eglantiere*, I was reluctant to endure another long-haul flight, preferring to remain home. Although managing and producing the magazine was time-consuming, it was not something I was keen to do while on holiday.

Two or three months at home by myself would also allow me the freedom to visit Timaru. I could care for my grandsons over *Queen's Birthday* weekend, while Jackie and Flash took part in the annual retro caravan weekend in Geraldine. There was also their forthcoming wedding in October to get excited about!

One other very important factor in staying home that year, was to oversee the installation of our new swimming pool. While a swimming pool was not on the check-list when we initially contemplated creating the place, it was more than a welcome addition.

In hindsight I missed out on a great opportunity to visit Brazil, as the person appointed to attend the *INF World Congress* to be held in Tambaba, decided not to go. Brian was asked if he would represent NZNF as their delegate. Needless to say, he jumped at the chance to attend. The Congress had never before been held at Brazil and by all accounts, it was a great success.

A flurry of activity followed Brian's return home only a few hours before Jackie and Flash were to be married in Timaru. If he was suffering from jet-lag, it wasn't in evidence, as we enjoyed a memorable family occasion before heading back north the following day, for another hot summer in Marlborough.

CloseUp program on TVOne pronounced Blenheim as enjoying the highest sunshine hours in the country and we were contacted by TVNZ reporter, Donna-Marie Lever, to see if we would take part in a short feature promoting Marlborough as the sunniest place in the country. Brian and I are no slugs when it comes to promoting ourselves, naturism, or our local region and were more than happy to invite the *CloseUp* crew to *Wai-natur*.

Donna arrived with super-large sunglasses for both of us to ward off the sun's strong rays and asked a few questions about our activities and how we felt about heading off Whakatane and Nelson with the highest sunshine hours. We agreed that Marlborough certainly has a great deal of appeal to visitors looking for a warmer climate.

She was a good sort, but looked hilarious stretched out on one of our loungers during the interview, clad from head to toe in black.

Kay and Brian being interviewed by Donna-Marie Lever for *CloseUp* on TVOne.

Imagine our delight when we viewed the program after the news and saw the owners from a local vineyard wearing similar eyewear. Best of all though, was a smiling Alistair Sowman, Marlborough District Mayor, strolling through Seymour Square in Blenheim, sporting the same ridiculous large sunglasses.

Nudie Foodies

Wairau Valley in Marlborough met all of February's climatic expectations, when naturists from Australia, UK, the Netherlands and New Zealand arrived at *Wai-natur* for the annual *Nudie Foodies Sounds Adventure*.

Nudie Foodies, if the truth were to be told, are the brainchild of Pete and Lesley Whalan, naturist friends and chefs extraordinaire, who have a passion for good food and wine. So much so, that their personalised number plate sports the words, *Nudie Foodies*.

Visitors at *Wai-natur* tend to take a low-key approach to happy hour and Friday's meet & greet saw small groups socialising around the shady gardens, sampling the habitual dip and crackers and sipping Marlborough's world renowned Sauvignon Blanc.

A few quiet sun lovers made the most of the late afternoon sunshine around the pool, while I worked on body maintenance, swimming continuously end to end of it for forty minutes. My daughter Jackie had travelled up from Timaru, especially to take care of the extra house-keeping required during the weekend. And, with a further six on-site caravans to service and more than our usual number of campers, she was kept pretty busy.

Fifty nudie foodies eagerly stepped up the pace the following morning to meet Aussie, skipper of *MV Odyssea*, a 20 metre luxury cat' at Havelock Marina, 40 minutes drive from *Wai-natur*. During the passenger check, a couple smilingly introduced themselves and presented vouchers for the *Green Shell Mussel Tour*. We could not help laughing as I called out to Chris Godsiff, owner of *Marlborough Travel* and skipper of the smaller *MV Spirit* moored alongside, 'We've got two of yours now, Chris'.

By 10:00am we were underway at a fast clip, heading into the Pelorus Sound. What an unexpected bonus to pull up alongside one of Marlborough's 550 mussel farms where Aussie informed us of Marlborough's famous green lipped mussels.

No sooner had he finished when his side-kick, Hamish, emerged from the galley with several large bowls of freshly steamed mussels, enhanced only by lemon wedges and a delicious Wasabi sauce on the side. Surprisingly, there were a number of visitors that had never tasted them and hadn't realised what they had been missing (or had eaten a tough mussel years ago).

Not so in this case. These were the crème de la crème of mussels, and I was thinking that the boxed lunch prepared by the *Wairau Valley School PTA* the night before would pale in comparison to this!

Meanwhile, in and around the three levels of the cat; nudie foodies were nudie cruisin', in awe of the majestic scenery of the Pelorus Sound. One of our visitors on a previous cruise, likened Jacob's Bay to a deserted island.

Aussie expertly moored *Odyssea* alongside the jetty with the help of Hamish, and advised that departure would be approximately 2:30pm, as the out-going tide would be earlier than normal. About half of the group opted to lounge around on board, the rest finding a grassy patch in the bay, to enjoy a blissful experience that only an afternoon in the Marlborough Sounds can afford.

In our dreams a long term stay would be ideal, but there was more in store for us yet.

There were two well formed tracks, each pointing in opposing directions. Not wishing to exert themselves after their packed lunch (which proved to be quite substantial), a number strolled up to the scenic lookout. The more energetic among us opted for the longer track (which led to Fairy Bay) where, eventually, we would dive off the back of the launch into the deep azure green waters. Even Hamish got his kit off and joined us skinny-dippers. Wow!

Everyone was in fine mettle while Aussie imparted his wide knowledge of the area as he guided us back to Havelock. Hamish was kept busy serving in the bar and we were all feeling pretty good on our return to *Wai-natur* in time for another swim in the pool, more flavoursome wines from the region and the first of a number of delicious canapés prepared by nudie foodie, chef du cuisine, Pete Whalan and his team; Lesley Whalan, Chris and Marty Matheson, Dave Care aka the bag boy, and Jackie.

Brian and a team of helpers set up the tables with white tablecloths and candles in a sheltered area of the garden festooned with coloured lights. Before long we were devouring an entrée of spicy chorizo with scallops. Guests were then served a main course with either duck breast or lamb rumps; followed by a mouth-watering dessert of lemon and fresh berries.

Nudie Foodies Sounds Adventure on board MV Odyssea; Kay with a bowl of delicious steamed mussels; Diana about to plunge into the Marlborough Sounds.

The previous year's Nude Golf International at the *Wairau Valley Golf Club* had been a great success and we were keen to have another tournament with the support of the community. Mindful of the number of school swimming pools closing throughout the country, due to lack of funds, we decided to do a little fundraising for the *Wairau Valley School* pool heating and maintenance.

One of our friends from the valley had donated a painting with the suggestion that a blind auction be held to further our cause. However the nudie foodies decided Kay and Brian should have it and the hat (or beret in this case) be handed round instead.

Sunday dawned and by 9:45am 16 players had teed off in the *Ambrose Tournament* at the scenic *Wairau Valley Golf Club*, a few minutes walk from Wai-natur. One hour later, a further 16 guests had boarded the *Grape Lander* luxury coach for a tour of Marlborough's wineries. Members of the *Wairau Valley School PTA* arrived at the golf club to serve morning tea and a hearty buffet lunch, while our next door neighbour, Tim, managed the bar and drove the drinks trolley around the course, ensuring none of us went thirsty.

The winning team appeared to be quite surprised but pleased, at their winning score and were presented with the grand trophy, which was first competed for at Lake Tekapo in 2002. Several sponsors from the valley and business associates of *Wai-natur* provided prizes for each player.

The total donation to the *Wairau Valley School PTA* of $725.00 included $300.00 from *Wai-natur,* $200.00 refund from golf club fees and a further $225.00 collected in the beret.

It was with a great deal of pride we received a thank you note from the *Wairau Valley School PTA*, together with a large number of beautifully crafted letters from the school's children which certainly enhanced our standing in our community.

Pete Whalan and Les Rootsey wait in the shade while Noel Thomas tees off during the Nude Golf International at the Wairau Valley Golf Club.

Invitation to a Wedding – in France

Pack only a small suitcase; sage advice for those taking a flight on any airline these days, particularly when commuting via London to any of the European destinations. I afforded a quiet smile at Heathrow as I sat calmly, flat white at hand, handbag secured by the left, contemplating several families; trolleys burgeoning with belongings, drunkenly weaving a path to Ryan Air or Jet Star check-in counters.

First up, a couple of three day stops with good friends in the Netherlands in Amsterdam, where I stayed with Onno and Martine, who had visited us during our first year at *Aoraki Naturally*, and coincidentally, our initial summer at *Wai-natur*. Then south to solid, dependable Rotterdam, where Elly has lived all her life. The contrast between these two large cities, barely 80kms apart, is fascinating. Amsterdam is full of must-see attractions, while Rotterdam appears only to cater to its burgeoning harbour trade. Elly ensured I saw a lighter side, with lunch at one of the numerous river-side restaurants.

Before long I was ensconced on the TGV fast train to Avignon. I don't believe anybody should miss out on the stunning scenery of Provence while visiting Europe and it provided an ever-changing panorama from my comfortable seat.

At the foot of the old Provençal village, Reillanne, between Forcalquier and Apt, hidden in a beautiful valley at an altitude of 350 meters, lies the naturist paradise, *Le Vallon des Oiseaux*. The 50 hectare site enjoys a Mediterranean Sea climate with more than 300 sunny days per year!

Now that's my kind of paradise.

My arrival at *Le Vallon* was not met with the usual bonhomie of owner Jan Pasma, as he was holidaying in Spain. He was to greet me later, during dinner on the terrace.

Opting for a second-story room in the spacious gite rather than an on-site van, I quickly settled in, took in the gorgeous view across the valley and then made a beeline for the expansive swimming pool. Ah bliss.

Meanwhile, Brian, who was across on the other side of France, working at *L'Eglantiere*, picked up our Peugeot rental the following morning and set off to join me. Later in the evening he was cooling off in his own fashion, with an Amstel beer. We were both delighted to see Jan's daughter, Amanda, once more. Many of our friends in New Zealand will remember her when she stayed at *Wai-natur* during the previous summer.

Surprisingly, Brian managed to stay in one place doing absolutely nothing apart from visiting the markets, for five days. Even more unexpectedly, he kept up this pace for the next five weeks. So it was in a very relaxed manner we travelled across the hills to stay at *Haut Chandelalar*, where several years before, we had enjoyed a couple of days R&R. The owners, Muriel and Ives, surprised us one summer by returning the visit at *Wai-natur*.

Refreshed, Brian stepped up the pace and we travelled south, immersing ourselves in French culture, visiting the hilltop village of Entrevaux with its mediaeval celebration and *St. Paul de Vence,* a short walk from the *Maeght Foundation*, an amazing modern art museum.

In sharp contrast, viewing within the *Chagal Museum* in Nice widened our perspective on religious art, though not our favoured theme. Although not our favoured city either, we found a lovely café deep within this city's narrow streets, before continuing our round trip which brought us to the *Perfumeries* at Grasse, where I managed to resist the lure of designing my own perfume.

Having reached the mid-way point of our holiday together, nevertheless we still had a great deal of ground to cover. The bag boy was currently domiciled in Le Puy-en-Velay, having helped at *L'Eglantiere* for a few weeks.

Though a little isolated, Le Puy-en-Velay is famous for being the starting point of one of the main pilgrim walks in France. Our fitness was tested climbing to the top of all three historical monuments, including a huge pink Mary and Jesus, visible from many parts of the town. The statue was made using metal from cannon seized during the Crimean war, and given to the town by Napolean.

After such exertion, our thirst was sated with a few pints of Guinness at one of two Irish Bars.

INVITATION TO A WEDDING – IN FRANCE

The three of us had accepted the invitation of Xavier and Isabelle to attend their wedding celebrations at a small village near Bordeux, on 3rd October 2009 and at their suggestion, we reserved accommodation at a nearby camping ground. This was quite a different experience for us, particularly meeting for pre-dinner drinks with other naturist friends from Holland, also invited to the wedding.

Our invitation also requested our presence at a luncheon prior to the wedding at the home of Isabelle's mother and partner; approximately 10kms away. Imagine our surprise on arrival, to see well over 60 family members and friends from 'far away' in the marquee, erected especially for the occasion.

Bride and groom, et al, were seated; then served a typical four course meal of the region, complete with wine and cheeses.

At the conclusion of the meal which was by no means hurried, we assembled en masse for photographs on the expansive grounds and were then given a small tulle bow and ribbon in the colours of the bride's ensemble, burgundy and cream, which we were instructed to attach to our car aerial. We had seen many cars with similar decorations during the past few years; an integral tradition in which we were more than happy to take part.

Our instructions were to follow the car in front. It was comical as several dozen cars tooted and waved their way over 10kms of countryside to their eventual destination, a car-park within walking distance of the town hall, where the civil ceremony was to take place.

Before we went any further, one of the guests donned a high-vis' jacket, and holding up traffic, directed the large group of guests to where the Maire was waiting patiently outside the building. Crowding into the office, surrounding the circle of seated bridal party and family, guests spilled out onto the pavement as the Maire read a section from the French constitution which lists the responsibilities that the couple will need to fulfil in their marriage. Of the two ceremonies in a classic French wedding, the civil one is the only one that is legal. We were wondering if that was it!

We were not disappointed, as the high-vis' jacket was again fastened securely, and the bridal procession guided to the Church nearby. By this time, guest numbers had swelled considerably, barely fitting into the Church decorated with burgundy and pearl helium balloons anchored with wide ribbons to each pew.

One would be forgiven for thinking that as a regular visitor to France I would have commanded much of the French language by now, but my lack of knowledge meant I could hardly understand a word during the thirty minute ceremony. Although, I hasten to add, this did not deter from my enjoyment, especially when a beautiful vocal arrangement was sung by all four children.

Traditionally in New Zealand, the bride and groom lead the family and guests out of the church. So, another surprise when I saw Xavier's parents, Marcelle and Maurice, arm in arm with Isabelle's mother and her partner, move toward the Church doors, followed closely by family and guests.

Some time later the happy couple eventually emerged to rousing cheers, as friends, armed with camp-chairs and all things camping, formed a guard of honour.

Then on went the high-vis' jacket again and we noisily proceeded along to the car-park, vehicles deferring to the entourage blocking the narrow streets with patient amusement. Yet again, the instruction to follow the car in front, led us, tooting and waving, to another small village, where we spilled out on to the entrance-way to a large building. This was where the reception was to be held.

Tables laid with white linen cloths were enticingly set out with flutes of champagne and a variety of canapés. We were informed that this was a welcome

Isabelle and Xavier Feraut cutting their wedding cake during the reception.

drink for all the friends who were not invited to the reception. Sunset signalled its conclusion, whereupon Isabelle lit a small bonfire decorated with colourful paper flowers. Legend has it the longer the fire burns, the stronger the marriage. It seemed to me that it burnt quite a while.

A board displaying dried grape-leaves and identifying several different varieties, directed us to our table, where we found a similar dried grape-leaf identifying us, our name painted in silver. It would be a while before we ate (thank goodness says she), as several guests lampooned Xavier and Isabelle with skits and power point presentations of their respective lives. This is the way they do it in France and I loved every minute of it.

I can't tell you what time they served the main meal. It was late and of course, like the wine on the tables, there was plenty of it. The band, led capably by a one-armed drummer, began playing at the conclusion of dessert, which was getting on for midnight. Brian and I, always ready for a twirl on the dance floor, attempted to compensate for the massive calorie intake of the previous few hours.

With a sober Brian at the wheel, we had gone full circle by the time we returned to the camping ground and fell into bed. Next morning, having packed up the car, we returned to the hall to help clean up. No sooner had we finished, than the tables were being covered in white paper and a buffet meal laid for the 50 or more friends and family members who had turned up to help.

We were anxious to get moving, as we were due to fly out of Toulouse the following day. With a nude photography workshop to be held in the spring and a magazine deadline of less than two weeks away, I was keen to get on the plane and back in my own bed in New Zealand.

Reluctantly, we bade farewell to an emotional Xavier and Isabelle. Brian gave me a hell of a scare as he turned left onto the roundabout instead of right and zoomed around the wrong way back into the car-park, winding down the window at the open-mouthed gathering of friends.

'I've always wanted to do that,' he laughed.

And with a final flutter of our *All Blacks* flag, we were off again, this time to the right.

If we showed some anxiety earlier, two hours later we were getting frantic about where we would stay overnight. We had hoped to stop at a gite in one of the villages along the way but large religious ceremonies were evident at this time, with crowds of cars and people blocking the roads.

Eventually we found a village which, by comparison, appeared deserted. I knocked on the first door of what I thought was a hotel, only to receive a blank.

'Maybe they are involved in the neighbouring celebrations,' I thought to myself.

As if on cue, a couple of burly gendarmes pulled up in a familiar blue van at the intersection. I scurried across the road, and asked them if they knew the owners of the hotel and could they help us? In the meantime, a young guy came out from behind the hotel on his motorbike, saw the gendarmes and shot back in again. Obligingly, one of the gendarmes gave a sharp rap on the hotel door, which in due course was opened by the owners.

Thinking the gendarme wanted to speak to their son – driving while underage – they were somewhat red-faced, but instead, our friendly gendarme explained our predicament. Upon which, the door was opened wide and we were welcomed into a very comfortable overnight stop.

Isabelle with her daughter Suzy in the sauna at *L'Eglantiere*

Figure Studies

Springtime in the valley . . . what better season to hold a nude photography workshop hosted by *Wai-natur Naturist Park* in Marlborough – one of the sunniest regions of New Zealand.

Having read about various nude photography workshops in other naturist magazines, I was excited about planning our own workshop. We had contacted a professional tutor and engaged a model through a reputable agency in Blenheim.

Prior to the workshop, I distributed a media release with information about the weekend event. In due course, Angela Crompton, a young journalist from the local *Marlborough Express*, telephoned with a request to interview me and I responded to Angela's questions in my usual frank manner.

Angela explained there was not enough time for a photographer to come and take a photo for her article, so asked me if I could provide one instead.

Kay poses by the pool at *Wai-natur*. Note: This photo was published in the *Marlborough Express*.

A suitable pose by the pool was deemed to be the most appropriate and emailed with the proviso;

'If you plan on putting black duct tape on or pixelating my nipples in anyway, I would rather you didn't publish it.'

To which the response was . . . 'well, the editor ummed and ahhed and said, "Let's publish it and see what the reaction is." '

Predictably, the reaction was provided by a lone letter to the editor, 'wondering what this pornographic photo was doing in our paper and that it was disgusting'.

A further flurry of letters to the editor showed plenty of support for our lifestyle and for the paper, with one writer providing the definition of pornography from the Concise Oxford Dictionary and criticizing the writer for their narrow-minded attitude to adult, healthy and totally harmless nudity in the 21st century.

Another wondered if they had ever bothered to think about the attitudes which result in the English-speaking world having such appalling outcomes for teenage pregnancy, abortion and STIs, when compared to countries such as Denmark?

Body shame has consequences and they are widespread and serious. Prudery is child abuse with good intentions.

Two powerful statements, which had the effect of complete strangers smiling at me during a visit to the supermarket the following week.

A number of workshop participants were residents of nearby Picton and Blenheim; others travelled some distance and stayed Friday and Saturday evening in our B&B and onsite caravans. Thought to be the first of its kind in New Zealand, the two day workshop allowed camera enthusiasts to unravel the mysteries of camera craft and create better figure studies.

Wai-natur is a stunning property in Wairau Valley and includes large stands of oaks, larches, birches and many other established specimen trees, plus a fabulous heated swimming pool - what better backdrop for nude photography!

Under the expert tuition of professional photographer, Roger Thwaites APSNZ, six camera enthusiasts from around New Zealand were guided in the art of nude portraiture. Following a 'meet & greet', Roger outlined the weekend's programme and presented an introduction to portraiture basics, including posing and composition. Jemimah then joined the group who then learnt this was Jemimah's first experience at modeling and being nude in the company of strangers. She proved to be a delightful subject and showed a confidence far beyond her experience and years.

Although inexperienced at nude photography; the six budding enthusiasts

FIGURE STUDIES

Jemimah strikes a pose in the garden during the nude photography workshop at *Wai-natur*.

under the expert tutelage of Roger and with the flexible co-operation of Jemimah, revelled in the opportunity to try out a variety of poses. Different foliage and textures in the garden afforded a wide raft of backgrounds for our model, and with two days in which to experiment with lighting and contrast, everyone was relaxed and enjoyed every minute of it. It was also wonderful to see each of the participants in the workshop assisting one another with the light-board and patiently standing aside in order for others to get the best shot.

During lunch and later, while everybody was enjoying a welcome afternoon tea in the shade, Roger talked about learning the various components and settings of cameras. These are as diverse as there are makes and models of cameras, he explained, but he encouraged participants to read their manuals and try each facet out; to take time and experiment how to get the best out of their cameras.

No nude photography workshop would be complete without some photos of our model in the pool. Of course our camera enthusiasts also made the most of the opportunity to have a swim before the day's end.

We are very lucky here in the valley to have a small number of friendly neighbours who are comfortable about our lifestyle. One of these allowed us the use of their vineyard which was just a short drive from *Wai-natur*. However the sun was very intense and by the time we arrived there on the Sunday morning, the light conditions were just not suitable, but the few trees provided some shade and interesting backdrops for our model. Also from there, we made a mental note to return in the autumn when the golden hues of the vines will afford optimum results.

Understandably, our course participants all agreed the weekend was a great success, with the majority requesting a follow-up course on nude recreation photography.

Naked Ambition

We had been members of the Marlborough Chamber of Commerce for a number of years and I finally agreed to General Manager, Brian Dawson's suggestion of entering the annual Business Excellence Awards.

Our entry would be submitted for the Marlborough Lines Powerhouse of New Zealand Business Award – for small businesses. Entrants would also be assessed for Environment, Technologies Innovation and Customer Service awards.

As was the case the previous year, Brian had travelled to France during the winter, while I enjoyed four months at home, with just Nud for company. These were special times for Nud and me as we walked several kilometres a week around the valley roads and the scenic golf course.

Having accepted the challenge, I read the entry form. And read it again and again and again until I could clearly understand the questions and could answer them in a clear and concise manner; a manner in which others would understand and more importantly, gain insight into the core values of our business.

Subjects covering management and strategy, marketing, environment, innovation, investing in people and skills, customer service, succession planning and of course the bottom line – financial success, required a written response of at least 500 words for each and in some cases charts and graphics to illustrate various features. Completing the project of 25 pages entirely on my own brought about another challenge. Would it pass scrutiny from others?

The best way to find out was to ask, and who better to ask than my sister, Sue.

Sue cast an expert and professional eye over my presentation and proof-read it into the bargain. It seemed it would pass muster and I registered our entry by the due date of 30th September.

As a bonus for entering the awards, PC Media made a 60 second video clip, screened the night of the Awards presentation. A profile was featured in the Chamber's magazine, Voice, and the Business Excellence Awards brochure, plus an acknowledgement in the Chamber's weekly email.

The *Marlborough Express* also featured a profile in the lead-up to the Awards.

'Just a small suitcase is required when visiting *Wai-natur Naturist Park* in Wairau Valley. Owners Kay Hannam and Brian Williams, say that birthday suits are 'de rigueur' this summer, accessorised with hat and sunnies to complete this season's fashion look.

Day visitors are welcome at this secluded and quiet campsite with all the amenities of a regular camping ground, with outdoor hot spa and fabulous solar heated swimming pool.

A visit to *Wai-natur Naturist Park* will not cause permanent harm to anyone. On the other hand, it may change your life. Experience the freedom for yourself.'

We were certainly receiving a great deal of free publicity.

Only days earlier Brian had arrived home and the usual flurry of activity began with the advent of Spring and warmer days ahead. The bag boy arrived home also – with Madeleine – from France.

Life sure looks interesting for the bag boy!

Apparently Brian had met Madeleine at *L'Eglantiere* the previous year. As *Artisan in Residence*, she and the young adults created all manner of artwork, even a small hut made out of mud and straw, sited alongside the picturesque river.

These two were smitten with one another and it looked as though we would have to find someone else to carry our bags.

Summer promised to be an exciting time for all of us.

Then it was the Awards night at a glamour Gala Dinner held in the *Marlborough Convention Centre*. Black tie meant a new dress for Kay, while Brian resurrected his jacket from the back of the wardrobe and sent it off to the dry-cleaners.

Needless to say, there was no show without punch and we welcomed Dave and Madeleine in the foyer for pre-dinner drinks with other entrants, sponsors, judges and board members of the Chamber.

No sooner had the entree been consumed when spot prizes and the first of the awards were presented. You can imagine the increased heart-rate when the presenter read out the name of the runner-up for the small business award;

Wai-natur Naturist Park. Understandably, I could not remove the smile from my face before, during, or after, my acceptance speech.

As if that wasn't enough excitement for the evening, following the main course, further awards were announced, including joint winners of the Environmental Award: *Clubs of Marlborough* and . . . drum roll . . . *Wai-natur Naturist Park*. Wow! Unbelievable!

The smile was still there and I was too excited to be nervous as I accepted the award on behalf of the team with Brian at my side, while the bag boy recorded the presentation on camera.

It gave me even greater pleasure to inform the 180 guests present . . .

'We naturists are environmental pioneers. The most significant factor in reducing our carbon footprint is choosing not to wear clothes. This means that we dispense with one of the most environmentally damaging components of our day to day consumerism – those fashionable short-lived clothes, as well as the associated laundry water and chemicals.'

There were more headlines and a photo of the three of us with Marlborough District Council Environment Committee Chairman, Graeme Taylor, in the *Marlborough Express* with the following caption:

Wai-natur Naturist Park – Joint Winner Marlborough District Council Environmental Award; Runner-up Powerhouse of New Zealand under $500,000 Business Excellence Award.

Graeme Taylor, Marlborough District Council Environment Committee Chairman, Kay and Brian, and Dave Care at the Marlborough Chamber of Commerce Business Excellence Awards. Photo by Frank Gasteiger.

It was extremely satisfying to note my final comments quoted in the awards coverage featured in the *Marlborough Express*.

'The naturist philosophy is based on respect: respect for ourselves, respect for each other and respect for the environment.'

Life is Short – Play Naked

Having owned and operated our own naturist accommodation business for the past fifteen years, it was inevitable that Brian and I would find it increasingly difficult to attend annual naturist rallies or festivals held in various clubs around the country. Occasionally one of us would stay home and look after things while the other managed to attend some or all of the week's festivities, but we were always mindful of the expectations of our visitors.

As with other holiday parks, the busiest time for visitors is just after Christmas and over the New Year period. No sooner does this group pack up and go back to work, and then another lot of holiday-makers start arriving. February brings out the dinks (double income no kids) and is our busiest month, with annual nude events being held mid-way through the month also.

No rest for the wicked – as the saying goes.

After a hiatus of several years, I made plans to attend *A Fairy Tale Circus.* This was the NZNF's sixtieth annual festival and was to be held at the *Auckland Outdoor Naturist Club.* I was excited about seeing many of my friends in one place again and it looked as though the program held plenty of variety. I ransacked my 'dress-up box' for something red to wear to the *Moulin Rouge* night and Oh! What to wear to the *Fairy Tale Ball*? Maybe the black cloak and hat would do?

Brent Thomson was the AONC Club President and as it had been some time since he and I met, I jokingly suggested he would probably recognise me as the wrinkly old witch. He knowingly responded he thought I was rather more the fairy godmother type.

That was easy and much more fun! I could recycle the Mardi Gras dress I made sixteen years ago (all that power walking and swimming had kept the love handles under control), add some wings, tiara and a wand and hey presto! I could pass muster as the fairy godmother.

With that in mind and in keeping with the 'fairy tale' theme, I requested a pumpkin be made available from the airport to transport the fairy godmother to the circus. Imagine my surprise when one of the members, complete with sparkly headwear, pulled up at the carpark in a flash convertible. Some pumpkin! With the top down and hair blowin' in the breeze I was ready for a week of sunshine!

Yeah right!

Of course the AGM was held the following day in the marquee, while everyone was outside enjoying what was to be the only day it didn't rain.

Even though my work with the magazine kept me very busy and in touch with the naturist community, it was felt I had considerable amount of experience to draw upon, and could assist with the upgrade of the federation website. With that in mind, I was duly elected back on the executive as South Island Vice President. Full of enthusiasm, I joined our newly elected Communications Officer, Donna Miller, and Internet Co-ordinator Wendy Chamberlain to prepare the initial scoping plan to refresh and renew the website.

I had been allocated a neat little retro caravan which was handily placed to the clubhouse and all the action in the marquee. And at quiet times I could, from the comfort of my bed, catch up on a spot of reading when I wasn't chatting with old friends, some of whom I had not met since Brian and I had first moved to Lake Tekapo.

With an abundance of clowns at every turn, there were plenty of smiles from the AONC team as they provided anything from hot pies to ice-creams. In fact all manner of nourishment and refreshment was available. The only time I left the club grounds was to take a walk around the neighbourhood.

Not only did the team meet the challenge of providing some pretty spectacular entertainment during the ensuing week, they competed with torrential downpours at times, forcing some in tents to just pack it all in, which was a real shame. I guess the thunderstorm during the 'meet & greet' did it. Many of us die-hard 'rally-goers' stripped off and partied on, but the continuous downpour was pretty demoralizing for some.

Apart from everything else, those who departed missed a fabulous catered dinner, followed by a mini opera performance. Side-shows were in evidence when the rain eased, and there was a great line-up of 'circus' performers during the annual concert.

New Year's Eve is always celebrated in grand style at any naturist festival. This year was no exception with several nursery rhyme and storybook characters, including Huckleberry Finn and a Cinderella or two arriving in the circus tent. Several OTT cross-dressers posed for the camera, raising just as many shrieks as the AONC's professional pyrotechnics crew, who – right on the stroke of twelve – let rip with a continuous stream of fireworks, providing a colourful spectacle to welcome in the New Year.

Of course I joined in the sports and played petanque, at times under an umbrella and as on previous occasions, we were all grateful for the dedication and patience of those who gave up their time to organise the competitions. Table tennis and bowls were played indoors. I passed on tenniquoits and volleyball – though others braved the wet slippery ground. With rather more enthusiasm than finesse, I played miniten – between showers. Even though I had not played for some years (and it showed), it was great to be back on the court again, having fun.

It brought back memories of my early forays on the miniten court and how each year at the end of the competition, several women who had played would get together for their annual photo shoot; *The Gems*. This tradition has continued for several years now and the photo serves as a reminder of the many wonderful women friends who employ a similar attitude towards fitness and health. Importantly, it also shows how comfortable we all are together, having participated in healthy outdoor exercise, free of clothing and without struggling with sweaty knickers or tight bras.

Life is short - play naked.

The Gems at Auckland Outdoor Naturist Club 2012. June, Margaret, Jude, Delwyn, Chris, Kay and Yanny. Photo by Conrad Inskip.

Julie at *L'Eglantiere,* France.

Festivals in France – Parks in Croatia

Brian, aka the 'Kiwi Chef', had his colourful pepper trousers packed, ready to depart early July. He was keen to be in a warm place, having experienced his first snow fall in the valley since leaving Lake Tekapo.

My own departure a month later, was a mad scurry to complete the September issue of *gonatural* magazine and despatch the file to the printer. With the 'to do' list completed, I was out the door and on the plane to Auckland where I was to meet up with my friend and NZNF Secretary, June Campbell-Tong.

Our chief destination was *Koversada* in Croatia, where June would attend the INF World Congress as NZNF Delegate, with Brian and I as observers. We were looking forward to reuniting with several of our naturist friends made during the past fifteen years.

Olympic fervour was evident, with several television 'media stations' throughout Singapore airport, broadcasting four different sports and with comfortable couches squared off around each. A pleasant manner for June and me to while away the hours between long haul travels.

Popping jet-lag and sleeping pills to help make it in the dark to Frankfurt, our arrival in Toulouse coincided with New Zealand's Nick Willis 'running on empty' in the 1500 metres. No such problem with our Peugeot 207SW with full tank and Brian at the helm. We sped off through the familiar countryside to our first destination, *Domain de L'Eglantiere*.

Julie, Remi and Suzy, whose photos have all graced the pages of *gonatural* magazine, now aged between 15 and 17, appeared to be twice as tall and certainly 'grown up', since the last time I saw them three years earlier, at their parents' wedding.

Having managed the busy Epicerie during previous summers at *L'Eglantiere*, I indulged in a week of sunshine, devouring several books, al fresco breakfasts and fresh local cuisine; exploring the local countryside (the highlight being the gondola trip up the Pic du Midi); lounging alongside the beautiful swimming pool and swimming my daily K, even showing up for the strenuous 5pm aqua exercise sessions.

Nearby, the *Marciac Jazz Festival* was underway, providing free entertainment by several international musicians. An early start ensured a seat in the plaza, adorned with huge shade sails courtesy *La Depeche*.

Venturing further, to Lupiac, we virtually 'stumbled' across the inaugural *Medieval Festival* celebrating D'Artagnan, Captain of the three mousquetairs. Practically everyone was costumed. A cardinal, bands, sword fights, felting, cheese-making, woven seats, and lace-making all contributed to a memorable afternoon.

Keen to meet up with the bag-boy, David, and Madeline, we headed for Foix. A marvel of 10th century architecture, the *Chateau de Foix* could be seen in the distance.

In the large central square of Mirepoix we admired the half-timbered houses supported on wood pillars, creating a magnificent covered arcade of fantastical sculptures in which a market was in full swing, tempting us to purchases otherwise not made.

On to the walled city of Carcassone and from Narbonne, Brian turned towards the Med' and *La Grand Cosse*, another favourite naturist resort, with its great pool complex and well organised campsite within a short walk over the dunes to the beach.

We had arranged to stay for a week in one of the super 'mobil-homes' owned by *Parasol Holidays*. It wasn't difficult to idle away a week at this very relaxed and friendly naturist site and we spent many pleasurable hours chatting and dining with the many British naturists who return each year. We managed to add a couple more days in order to join one of their weekly nights at a local vineyard restaurant, also to visit the seven locks of *Ecluses de Fonséranes* on the Canal du Midi west of Béziers.

Meanwhile, Brian aka 'Possum' by back-seat drivers, due to his tendency to drive fast, causing the aforementioned passengers to loll drunkenly around the back seat, had consumed the right amount of caffeine and was itching to be someplace else.

That 'someplace else' was *Domaine le Romegas*, a holiday centre located in the Drôme provençale, near the picturesque town of Buis-les-Baronnies and which boasted, 'an exceptional natural environment.'

Nestled in a wide, steep valley, *Romegas* sprawled across 100 acres, positioned to take advantage of the late afternoon sun.

Directed to a dirt road well above the camping line, we settled in one of several groups of maisonettes. Of minimalist design with small bathroom, double bed and bunks for the three of us and kitchen adjacent to a small enclosed terrace.

Breaking in new country behind Mont Ventoux, 'Possum' led us once more to one of the most beautiful naturist resorts in Provence: *Le Vallon des Oiseaux*, owned by our old friend Jan Pasma and his lovely daughter Amanda.

As usual, we were treated royally with separate upstairs rooms in the gite. *Le Vallon* has a wonderful ambience.

June and Kay enjoy lunch al fresco; Kay and Brian on the Beach at *La Grand Cosse;* Jan Pasma at *Le Vallon des Oiseaux.*

Not too big, nor too small. An interesting landscape as the name suggests, situated in a beautiful valley, plus a colourful family of feathered friends.

The reception/bar/restaurant/terrasse is both quiet and busy, depending on the occasion and Jan is still as gregarious as when we first met him in 2000. As is often the case, the 'collective meal' was the highlight of the week, with Brian in his element, preparing salads.

We were keen to see more of the surrounding region. Roussillon is lovely from the outside, set in a deep green pine forest on bright red-ochre hills. It's even more spectacular inside the village, with colourful old buildings and narrow medieval streets.

Having visited Roussillon on a previous occasion, we were reminded how steep and narrow the streets were, so dropping June off at the top of the village centre seemed a good idea. Finally we found a pay parking area right down at the bottom before locating a steep passageway, which we agreed would bring us somewhere within 'cooee'. It took us about twenty minutes wandering the streets to eventually locate June at one of her favourite holiday pastimes, street markets!

We had heard a great deal about Gordes; one of the most well known hilltop villages in the Luberon. The imposing Chateau dominating large clusters of stone houses 'growing' on the hillside; the labyrinth of narrow streets begging to be explored. The reward - a stunning photography exhibition, held alongside an expo of beautifully crafted national costumes down through the ages. Our first ever taste of lavender ice-cream completed our excursion.

With our little Peugeot packed to the gunnels, we were off again; sent on our way with the usual trumpeting from Jan. And within a few hours we were accommodated in well appointed cabins at *Le Betulle*, glancing anxiously at the sky above – in Italy.

Next morning, braving the weather and with GPS assistance, our Peugeot was conveniently parked in the CBD of nearby Torino. Boy! Did it rain! Torino has several interesting museums and palaces to find shelter and explore.

It was too far for Brian to drive to Ancona in one hit, so we settled on an overnight stop at Faenze – a delightful town. The ensuite bedrooms weren't too bad either. June and I indulged in some 'retail therapy' and had fun trying and buying, before finding Leone Conti, a small organic vineyard on the outskirts of town, owned by a young Italian winemaker and his American wife, who produce many diverse wines; all of which represent their pursuit for the ideal harmony between wine and emotions.

Researching online, June had made a reservation for *The Beautiful Farmhouse*. It was raining heavily by the time we arrived and our accommodation turned out to be a little log cabin close by *The Beautiful Farmhouse*. But the food was to die for and plenty of it. So it wasn't all bad.

A sedate overnight ferry crossing from Ancona was less challenging than anticipated, and we were glad to feel the warmth of the Croatian sun on arrival in Split. A quick recap and we were off to Dubrovnik, 'the city of a million steps' or so it seemed, when faced with access to and from our rooms. The owners offered a garage in which to park the Peugeot while we got to grips with the local bus service.

Shortly after we purchased tickets to climb around the wall of the old city, an horrific thunderstorm hit. We had been advised that once we came down off the wall, that was it! We battled on for another hour, until eventually, soaked to the skin, we found shelter in a warm, crowded café.

Evidence of the recent war was everywhere, none more poignant than the museum accessed by gondola on the hill opposite the old city and travelling through countryside punctuated with houses riddled by bullets, sometimes homes remodelled but unfinished, due to the lack of able bodied menfolk, was a chilling reminder of what had gone before.

Picturesque Trigor, with it's cacophony of bells ringing on the hour and a beautiful apartment booked by June, ticked all the right boxes for us. While enjoying an evening drink in the square, an entertaining local wedding took place in the church alongside.

Understandably, we were loath to leave this beautiful part of Croatia. However the best was yet to come.

Plitvice Lakes – the largest national park in Croatia – boasts more than 16 lakes, with dozens of waterfalls cascading into the clear azure waters. The park is registered as a UNESCO World Heritage site, covering more than 73,000 acres. Our downstairs apartment in a large roadside house was situated on the main highway, 5kms from the park.

Determined to see as much of the park as possible, we fronted up at the ticket office shortly after it opened in the morning. As we strolled around the wide, well maintained tracks and boardwalks, I expressed how lucky we are in New Zealand, that we can enjoy many of our own national parks unfettered by clothing; just a hat and a pack.

Koversada is the most famous naturist park on the Adriatic and one of the oldest in Europe; consisting of a campground, apartments and villas. It was here the 33rd INF World Congress was to take place. Luckily for us we chose to take a dip in the sea on the afternoon we arrived before exploring the vast resort, as the ensuing days seemed to be packed with meeting others; the Congress beginning two days later.

Kay and June at the INF World Congress at *Koversada*, Croatia.

Reuniting with our old friends, it was also a pleasure to finally meet the bubbly Federation of Canadian Naturists, President Karen Grant, having communicated with her during the past four years since she agreed to be our *gonatural* 'cover girl' when Brian attended the Congress in Brazil.

Late summer weather at *Koversada* can be tricky and the evening prior to the Congress, a massive storm wiped out all power, with the added consternation of the Congress getting underway the following day without the benefit of translators!

All our meals were provided at one of the large restaurants where one evening, young people dressed in traditional costume provided after dinner entertainment with Croatian National Dancing.

With his caffeine level maintained on a regular basis, 'Possum' returned us safely to *Le Betulle*. Only this time, owner Gianfranco Ribaldi was on hand to greet us; eager to host his friends from 'down-under' and apologetic he was unable to impress us with pizzas from his super duper Pizza oven. An international group of French, Dutch, Italian and New Zealand joined together for a typical Italian meal.

Traversing the Col de Montgenevre, 1850 metres high, to Briancon, led us into Provence. At the foot of Mont Ventoux, *Belezy* is a well recognised naturist resort where our British friends Tony and Diana, have a static van. We were keen to meet up and arrange to have dinner with them the following evening.

Establishing ourselves in our little maisonette, we headed off to the familiar large pool complex before booking a meal in the restaurant.

Belezy is like a small village and we soon spotted another little Peugeot, only to find they were members of *Wai-natur*! I don't know who had the biggest surprise; us or them.

Eventually, we returned to *L'Eglantiere* to recharge after the long drive and repack for the long haul flights ahead. Our last night in the restaurant was a delicious four course meal, including *Maigret du Canard* prep'd and barbecued to perfection indoors by both French and our very own Kiwi Chefs. Long dinner tables were beautifully laid out in the restaurant and the three of us (when Brian finally joined us) made the most of our special place with 'family Feraut'.

'Let's buy a new tent' says Brian before slipping into a deep sleep on board the A380.

'Then next year, we can afford to stay longer!'

Nothing is Better

Spring seemed to be wetter around the country than normal and the days in between showers were pretty warm. As Brian coped with never-ending growth outside, I knuckled down to clear the decks indoors.

I was quietly thankful Stephane Deschenes from Canada had been elected to the INF Committee instead of me. Although I was up for the challenge of liaising with other non-European countries, delegates had pretty wide expectations for the position. There was more than enough to keep me occupied here.

Ensuring our entry for the 2012 Business Awards made the deadline of 30th September, we then made sure all was in order to welcome Chamber members to our first ever *Business After 5*. Our visitors were understandably impressed with our grounds and naturally curious to find out more about *Wai-natur* and the reasons why so many naturists enjoy our facilities.

Interestingly, one of the topics discussed at the recent Congress in Croatia, was the benefits of liaising with non-naturist organisations. I quietly congratulated ourselves on our attitude toward our ever increasing network of businesses. We were getting to be old hands at this.

In order to get to know our neighbours a little better and to introduce new residents in the valley, we invited a number of locals to a neighbourhood brunch. Springtime is an ideal time and before long there were several neighbours trooping around our garden, many returning with treasures for their own.

Although our involvement in the neighbourhood is somewhat spasmodic, one of my personal highlights is judging the art at the Wairau Valley School Pets Day. As an onlooker, it brings back memories of parading with the pipe band at various regional A & P shows held around South Canterbury each year.

While we didn't excel at the business awards as we had the previous year, nevertheless we made the most of the opportunity given to promote ourselves in the lead up to the glitzy Awards night. Over 300 packed the Marlborough Convention Centre and we were in awe of the calibre of entrants. They were equally intrigued of us.

Encouraged to enter the Marlborough Environment Awards – a separate regional event – provided a valuable opportunity to put forward our ideas on sustainable management and also to expand on the definition of naturism.

'Naturism is a way of life in harmony with nature, expressed through social nudity, linked to self-respect, tolerance of differing views, together with respect for the environment.'

Judging was a far longer process, with a visit from all three judges. Valuable feedback was also provided and which we have placed on our website. The 32 entrants were also given an opportunity to tell their story in a slide show compiled by the awards trustees and shown during a celebration dinner at the Marlborough Convention Centre on 1st March 2013.

The perception of many toward social nudity is that it may be obscene or a criminal offence. There is no law in New Zealand that expressly bans nudity in a public place, so simple nakedness is not grounds for prosecution. However, complaints have to be investigated in case they turn out to be a matter of indecent exposure or offensive behaviour, more particularly having 'intentionally and obscenely exposed any part of his/her genitals'.

Police News February/March 2012.

The case against Nick Lowe is an example:

Nick was convicted of offensive behaviour and fined $200 and $130 costs after he was stopped by police while riding his bike nude on Akatarawa Rd, north of Upper Hutt, on 15th March 2009, the same day as the World Naked Bike Ride.

A female motorist had complained to police after seeing him pedal past in a state of undress – except for his legally required helmet. She later told the court she was 'fairly disgusted' when she saw him.

Nick Lowe - The Naked Cyclist.

Nick appealed the conviction to the High Court.

His lawyer, Michael Bott, had argued that public attitudes to nudity had changed and said Mr Lowe, who regularly trains in the nude, had not received any other complaints.

In his ruling, Justice Denis Clifford said Mr Lowe's nakedness had not met the test of offensive behaviour and quashed the conviction and fine.

However, he said the judgment did not mean that nude cycling could not constitute offensive behaviour in other circumstances in which it could cause anger, resentment or disgust.

In other words; social nudity is a matter of time, place and circumstance.

Towards the end of the season I reviewed the myriad of media reports and reflected on the shifts of public opinion towards social nudity in this country.

So is there another shift?

My intuition suggests there is. A spike in visitors to our website is a key indicator, as are a growing number of visitors, particularly those in a younger demographic, who return to stay again and again.

This season, visitors to *Wai-natur* are again more than the previous year. Due to the world wide recession, plus the high value of our dollar, the percentage of overseas visitors has dropped but domestic visitors have increased. I can see this trend continuing with the ground swell of support from others, especially when I read reports that more than 500 people helped smash the world record for skinny dippers here in New Zealand. Unsurprisingly, there were thousands of spectators who turned out to see them.

Traversing from simple nudity to social nudity may seem like a giant leap, but all it takes is the initial courage to dip your toe in the water. Now that they have experienced the exhilaration of plunging naked into the ocean with hundreds of other similarly unclad bathers, many of these brave skinny dippers will search for other opportunities to be naked. Even those seemingly voyeuristic onlookers may have a paradigm shift in their thinking.

During a day spent boulder-hopping down Saw Cut Gorge, the other couple of dozen hikers on the trail were seemingly unfazed by the five of us wearing nothing but hats. We struck up a conversation with several, including a family from Arizona now resident in Blenheim, as we criss-crossed this impressive gorge. After wading through deep, cool streams sensibly carrying our clothes on backpacks above our heads, we were basking in the sunshine, enjoying our lunch. Imagine our amusement when we spotted

Clockwise from top right: Brian and Kay at *Wai-natur*, photo by Scott Hammond, *Marlborough Express;* Jean and Margo relax by the pool at *Wai-natur* while Nud waits patiently for them to throw his stick; Madeleine working in the garden; Kay, Jean and Margo traverse a deep passage in the gorge, Photo Dave Care; Dave, Madeleine, Jean and Margo enjoy lunch in the sun in Saw Cut Gorge, Marlborough, Photo Dave Care.

a family heading our way and seeing inquisitive youngsters being herded ahead, while Mum and Dad peered over large rocks, surreptitiously taking a few holiday snaps.

In a New Zealand television program, 'How normal are you?' it was determined that one in every seven New Zealanders likes being naked. This means there are several hundred thousand people who may be looking for a congenial venue to be without clothes.

I take great pleasure in welcoming couples of all ages, often initiated by the male partner, comfortable in his own skin, wishing his wife shared his same relaxed attitude. By allowing his wife to experience those feelings herself and in her own good time, the attitude is shared and their relationship enriched.

How good is that?

These same couples, now regular visitors to Wai-natur, delight in telling me that they now feel complete relaxation in a social nude setting. They are unable to tell me of any other comparable social situations which provide the same degree of relaxation they have found to exist at a naturist park.

My life is far from extraordinary, but there are occasions when I arouse a curious response from others. There are a few who, at first unsure what a 'naturist park' is, smile knowingly when I explain that you only need a small suitcase when visiting.

Some appear embarrassed when faced with the realisation that I spend a large part of my life naked, and cannot get to grips with the scenario of carrying out normal everyday activities in the nude. All it takes is the right attitude – nude with attitude.

Websites

Wai-natur Naturist Park   www.naturist.co.nz
New Zealand Naturist Federation   www.gonatural.co.nz
International Naturist Federation   www.inf-fni.org